REVISED EDITION

W9-DGO-647

MAKE YOUR

Scanner

A GREAT DESIGN & PRODUCTION TOOL

MICHAEL J. SULLIVAN

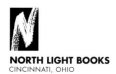

NORTH LIGHT BOOKS
CINCINNATI, OHIO

About the Author

Michael J. Sullivan is director of catalog design at Open Market Inc., based in Cambridge, Massachusetts. Formerly he was chief creative officer at Waypoint Software. He still maintains an interest in Haywood & Sullivan, a design/publishing firm operated by his wife and partner, Liz Haywood.

Holding degrees in both design and computer science, he is a regular contributor to design and computer-related design publications, such as *HOW* and *Publish*. He is also a regular lecturer at Seybold Seminars, the *HOW* Conference and other design-related conferences.

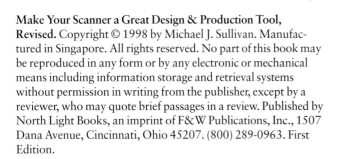

Make Your Scanner a Great Design & Production Tool, Revised. Copyright © 1998 by Michael J. Sullivan. Manufactured in Singapore. All rights reserved. No part of this book may be reproduced in any form or by any electronic or mechanical means including information storage and retrieval systems without permission in writing from the publisher, except by a reviewer, who may quote brief passages in a review. Published by North Light Books, an imprint of F&W Publications, Inc., 1507 Dana Avenue, Cincinnati, Ohio 45207. (800) 289-0963. First Edition.

Other fine North Light Books are available from your local bookstore, art supply store or direct from the publisher.

02 01 00 99 98   5 4 3 2 1

Library of Congress Cataloging-in-Publication Data

Sullivan, Michael (Michael J.).
Make your scanner a great design & production tool/Michael J. Sullivan.—Rev.
p. cm.
Includes index.
ISBN 0-89134-841-7 (alk. paper)
1. Computer graphics. 2. Scanning systems. I. Title.
T385.S82 1998   97-34611
006.6—dc21   CIP

Revision edited by Lycette Nelson
Production edited by Jennifer Lepore

The permissions on page 157 constitute an extension of this copyright page.

Introduction

This book assumes you have a scanner, scanning software and access to some sort of image-editing software (for color correction, cropping, rotating, eliminating dust and scratches, etc.) and that you know how to install the above items.

Throughout this book I refer to Adobe Photoshop and its filters and effects when I am talking about image-editing software. I do this for two reasons: First, Photoshop is the most widely used professional-quality image manipulation product on the market; second, it is also the most widely copied. Thus, products such as Corel Photo-Paint have most of Photoshop's commands (and then some). In addition, most software now supports Photoshop's plug-in architecture. A scanning plug-in that works in Photoshop also works with Fractal Design Painter. In short, Photoshop has become the lingua franca of the scanning world. If your software doesn't have a certain feature mentioned here, then you may need to figure out a work-around. In either case, I have made an effort to only show techniques that I feel either are or should be universal in any scanner repertoire.

Credits and Acknowledgments

All photographs used in this book, with the exception of those used in chapter four, Salvaging a Faded Original, and where otherwise noted, are © 1997 Michael J. Sullivan.

The image of Olé No Moiré is courtesy of Adobe Systems, Inc. The diagram How a Scanner Works is courtesy of Agfa Division, Miles Inc. The borders and clip art examples on pages 112 and 113, as well as the high resolution line art example on page 102, are from a turn-of-the-century type and ornaments spec book from an unknown publisher (the cover had been destroyed). The line art examples on pages 110 and 111 were scanned from *Americans* drawn by Charles Dana Gibson, printed by R.H. Russell, Publisher, New York in 1900.

Thanks are in order to my North Light Books editors, Lycette Nelson, Poppy Evans and Mary Cropper.

Thanks also for the invaluable help and enlightenment I received from the following individuals: Bob Schlowsky, Mike Owen, Ed Granger, Melody Haller, Steve Hollinger, François Gossieaux, Nancy and John Olson and Guy Jarvis.

Much love and admiration goes to my patient and supportive wife, Liz, and my daughter, Megan, who did without her dad for so many weekends.

This document was created electronically using QuarkXPress 3.2, Adobe Photoshop 3.05, Adobe Illustrator 6.0 and Adobe Acrobat Exchange 2.0 on Apple Power Macintosh computers. Flat artwork was captured using either an Agfa Arcus Plus or Epson Expression 636 scanner. 35mm slides were captured using a Polaroid SprintScan. Line conversions were produced using Adobe Streamline and saved as EPS files.

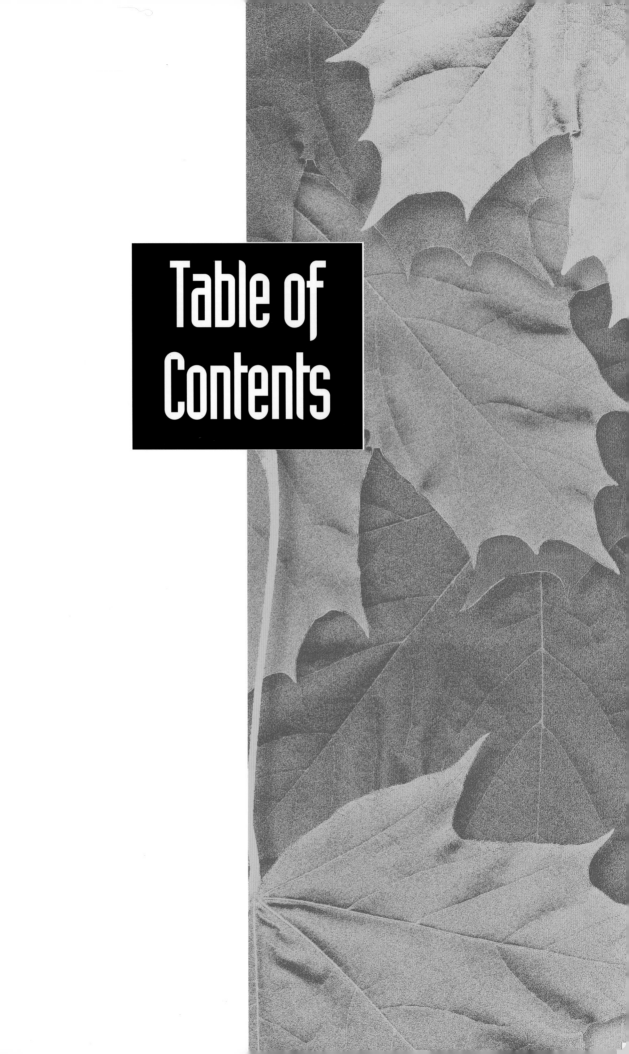

Table of Contents

CHAPTER ONE

Scanning

WHAT IT IS, WHAT IT DOES

The Scanner as an Input Device

The scanner is simply a gadget for getting images into your computer. That's it. But as you probably know, getting good images from your scanner requires more forethought and expertise than simply scanning them into your computer.

For one thing, getting good results requires knowing how to correct images with the tools in an image-editing program. However, this book is not about image manipulation techniques, per se. (If you want to become a Photoshop wizard, please see the Suggested Reading section in chapter five.)

Plus, you'll find that not all images can be "fixed" in an image-editing program. The old saying "garbage in, garbage out" applies to scanned images. It's far better to "fix" images at scan time than to try to fix them later in Photoshop or your favorite image-editing program.

To some degree, great scanned images are also the result of good equipment. This explains why your images don't look as good as the professionally scanned images you see in magazines and brochures. It's clearly due to the high-end equipment that publishers can afford to use.

Although great chefs can usually be found in great kitchens, they can also perform their art under less-than-ideal conditions. Even though you may "only" have an entry-level flatbed scanner, you can still achieve stunning results with it.

If you want to make the most of your equipment, optimize your scanning time and deliver the best possible images, then this book is for you! You'll find your scanner can be a really valuable tool when you know how to get good results from it.

How Scanners Work

The scanner is an electro-optical device that captures image data one line or "scan" at a time, hence the name. Using optics much like a camera's, a scanner moves over the imaging area, called the bed, which is defined by a grid of (x,y) coordinates. Each (x,y) coordinate defines a sample area, and the resulting captured image is described in samples per inch (spi).

Each sample is exposed to a light source of a known intensity. The light either passes through (in the case of a transparency) or is reflected from (in the case of artwork) an original. This light then makes its way through the optics of the scanner to a sensor, which converts the light to an electrical charge. The strength of the charge is in direct proportion to the intensity of the light, which is a reflection (no pun intended) of how light or dark the original sample is. The electrical signal is then converted to a digital signal using an analog-to-digital converter. It is this digital information that makes up the data in your scan.

Since each individual scan line must be calculated separately, scanners are not used to capture moving objects—the scanner is not a camera. But you can use a scanner much as you would a camera to capture 3-D artwork.

For more information see Scanning 3-D Objects on page 84.

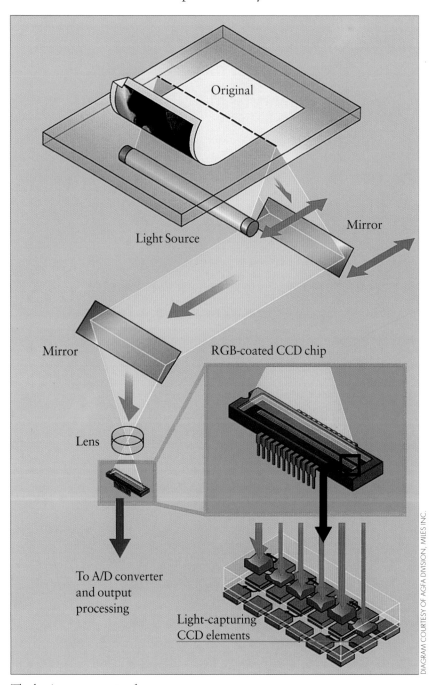

Original

Light Source

Mirror

Mirror

RGB-coated CCD chip

Lens

To A/D converter and output processing

Light-capturing CCD elements

DIAGRAM COURTESY OF AGFA DIVISION, MILES INC.

The basic components of a scanner.

Scanning and Its Relationship to Output

Halftone screens came about as a way to print, in four color and in black and white, the tone gradations that appear in photographs and illustrations. Halftone screens consist of many spots in varying degrees of concentration. In black-and-white or one-color printing, the concentration of spots is 100 percent for solid black or a solid area of color. A white area, or area of no color, is represented by a spot concentration of 0 percent. The range of spot concentration in between varies from 1 percent in the lightest regions of an image to 99 percent in the darkest.

Four-color reproduction is similar in that the four process colors (cyan, magenta, yellow and black) are combined in spots of various concentrations to yield an array of colors and tones. Each color in a printed image is the result of a blend of four halftone screens—one for each of the four process colors.

In the reproduction of digital images, three factors must be considered:

- The image's output resolution as defined by the number of dots per inch (dpi). 300 dpi is typical of laser printer output to plain paper, whereas service bureau imagesetters typically output images on photosensitive paper or film at a resolution of 1,200 or 2,400 dpi.

- Spot concentration, ranging from 0 to 100 percent as explained earlier.

- Halftone or screen frequency as measured in lines per inch (lpi). This term may

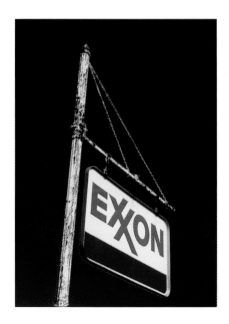

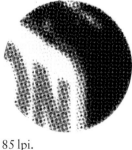 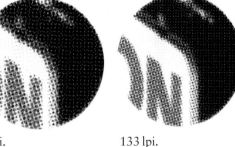 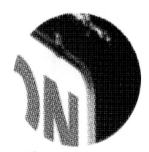

85 lpi. 133 lpi. 150 lpi.

A detail of the Exxon sign at 85, 133 and 150 lpi shows the difference in screen frequencies.

seem confusing because it doesn't describe lines per se, but rather the number of rows of spots that make up a halftone screen. The lower the frequency or number of rows, the coarser an image appears. Conversely, the higher the frequency, the more refined the image is.

Clearing Up the Confusion Among spi, dpi, lpi and ppi

Basic to understanding scanning and printing images is a knowledge of the terminology involved. As I researched other resources for this book, it became clear to me that no one in the industry was consistent in using terms to describe the resolution of scanned images. Many publications use the term *dpi* to describe the scan data, only to use the same term to describe the resolution of the output device—inconsistent and confusing, to say the least. Others use the term *ppi* (pixels per inch) to describe scanned data, a term that is also used to describe a computer's screen resolution.

In this book I have chosen to use the term *spi* (samples per inch) to describe the *scan data*. In essence, spi is the input frequency used when scanning the original. I also use the term to describe the frequency of the sample data when an image is scaled at output time. For example, although an image may be scanned and saved at 300 spi, when it is scaled to 50 percent of its original size in a page layout program, its effective sample frequency becomes 600 spi.

Because samples are not the same as laser printer dots, halftone spots or computer screen pixels, all other such prepress and desktop publishing terms (such as dpi, lpi and ppi) are used to describe output.

For more information see Best Screen Frequencies by Output on page 29.

Recommended Settings for Line Art Scanning

TERM	MEANING	DESCRIPTION	TYPICAL MEASUREMENTS
SPI	Samples Per Inch	Input Frequency of Scanned Image	300-1,200 spi (flatbed) 1,850-4,000 spi (slide)
DPI	Dots Per Inch	Resolution of Imagesetter (output)	300-2,400 dpi
LPI	Lines Per Inch	Halftone Frequency for Printer (output)	65-150 lpi
PPI	Pixels Per Inch	Resolution of Computer Screen (output)	72-96 ppi

This chart defines the various terms and typical output frequency for each.

The Scanning Process

The following is a step-by-step overview of the scanning process:

Step 1: Preview

Previewing lets you see a quick, small-scale version of the image before committing to the final scan. At this stage, you also see a frame or marquee around the image. You can adjust this frame to crop in on the portion of your image that you wish to scan.

Step 2: Crop to Desired Size and Shape

It's important to crop an image before scanning as opposed to after in your image-editing or page layout program. Cropping at the scanning stage reduces the amount of time needed to scan. Cropping also determines the way your image will look by confining the area in which the scanner's tone controls sense the darkest and brightest areas of the image.

Step 3: Decide on Input Mode: Line Art, Halftone, Grayscale or Color

LINE ART (also called 1 bit or bitmapped) is the best mode for scanning pure black-and-white originals, such as drawings, logos, signatures, etc. Line art should be scanned at the same resolution as the final output device to obtain maximum detail.

HALFTONE (or **DITHERED**) is used for scanning black-and-white photos or color photos to output in tonal gradations from black to white. This mode is a 1-bit format that simulates shades of gray by either creating halftone spots, halftone lines or diffusion patterns. This option is typically used for final output to low-resolution black-and-white laser printers. The high-resolution imagesetters that are found at service bureaus output grayscale images as described in step four. Halftone scans cannot be reverted to grayscale mode.

GRAYSCALE is the best mode for producing a black-and-white image with a realistic tonal range of grays. Its 8-bit continuous tone configuration produces 256 variations of gray for each sample and provides the greatest flexibility when working with black-and-white images. It's used primarily for producing black-and-white photographs and film negatives.

COLOR is the mode to select when working with a color image or when colorizing a black-and-white image. Its 24-bit continuous-tone configuration produces 256

Scanning for Output Method

This 200-spi, 8-bit grayscale scan gives you the greatest flexibility. It can be colorized, posterized and otherwise manipulated to your heart's content. However, images scanned in grayscale mode generally result in larger files than other black-and-white modes.

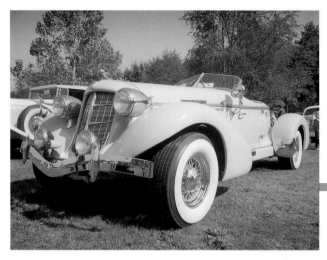

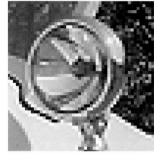

516K

Scanning the same image as a 1-bit halftone results in a dithered pattern where small black dots represent the various shades of gray.

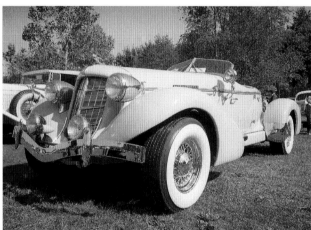

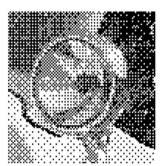

264K

Threshold scanning is useful when you want the unique look of a high-contrast image. Many designers use this effect for backgrounds and other graphic elements.

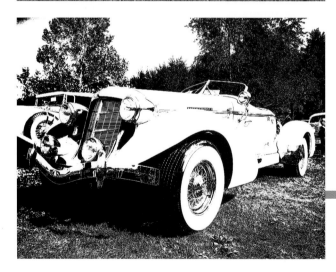

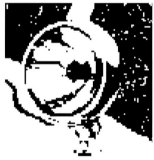

264K

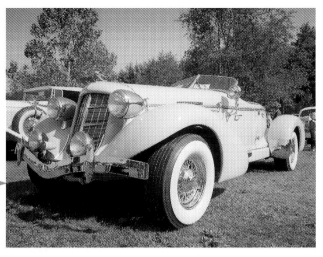

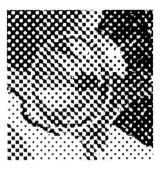

When output as a 75-lpi halftone at 600 dpi, this grayscale scan reproduces beautifully as a continuous-tone halftone.

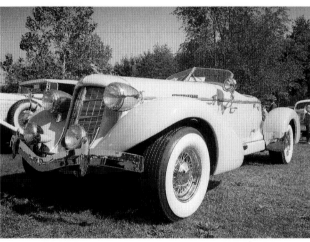

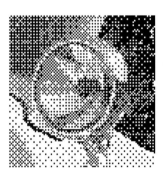

When output at 1,200 dpi this dithered image looks almost as good as the 75-lpi halftone. You may think that because it's a 1-bit image you have a smaller file, but that's not the case. Since this image required twice as many samples per inch as the corresponding grayscale image, it resulted in a file size comparable to that of the grayscale version.

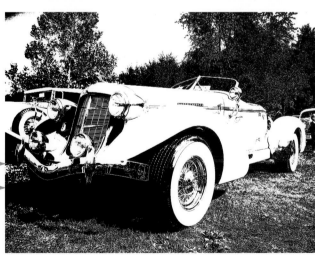

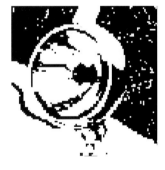

Scanned at 400 spi and output at 1,200 dpi, this 1-bit threshold image achieves a fairly high degree of detail. However, bear in mind that you can achieve the same high-contrast effect by bringing grayscale images into most page layout programs.

variations of each of three colors—red, green and blue (RGB)—for a total of 16,777,216 possible colors per sample (256 x 256 x 256). It's used primarily for producing color photographs and slides.

Step 4: Decide on Input Resolution (spi) and Scale

In chapter five you'll find tables on pages 145-147 to help you determine the proper calculations needed for optimal spi/scale settings. You may also want to try my online scan calculator at http://www.hsdesign.com/scancalc. However, here are some general guidelines you can follow for the various input modes.

LINE ART Output should be a multiple of the sample rate because the imaging data is sent directly to the laser printer or to the imagesetter's image engine. A 300-dpi laser printer needs line art at a resolution of 300 spi or 150 spi (a multiple of 300). For output to a 1,200-dpi imagesetter, scan at 300, 600 or 1,200 spi. You are limited in scaling this image in a page layout program if the resolution of the scaled image is not a multiple of the final dpi output. But the obvious advantage of using line art mode is that it produces a much smaller file than an image scanned in grayscale or color mode.

For more information see Scanning Fine Line Art on page 110.

GRAYSCALE An spi setting of 1.41 to 2 times output frequency is usually the maximum you should scan. For example, a grayscale image that will be output to 150 lpi (regardless of the output resolution of the laser printer or imagesetter) should be scanned at 212 to 300 spi.

COLOR As for grayscale, an spi setting of 1.41 to 2 times output frequency is the maximum you should scan. Because an RGB color file is three times the size of the same version of the image scanned in grayscale mode, keep the image resolution as low as possible without compromising quality.

NOTE: For permanently archiving grayscale and color images, scanning at the highest possible resolution (300 to 600 spi or more) is advised. You can resample the image to a lower resolution in an image-editing program when the image is retrieved.

The right scanning resolution and scale for an image also depend on its ultimate destination.

HIGHEST RESOLUTION SAMPLING As mentioned before, scanning at a high resolution is important when archiving an image. You should also scan at a high resolution when outputting an image on a larger scale. For example, a 600-spi scan delivers 300 samples per inch when output at 200 percent of its original size. Conversely, a 300-spi scan delivers 600 samples per inch when output at 50 percent of its original size. Ultimately, your computer's power and speed determine how large a file you can work with. An 8" x 10" (20.3cm x 25.4cm) color image, scanned at 300 spi (a 2-to-1 sample rate) for 150-lpi output at 1,200 dpi results in a 21.6MB file. Not every computer can handle files this big!

OPTIMAL RESOLUTION SAMPLING This sampling gives the best possible results for your image's output destination at a resolution that doesn't result in an enormously large file. You can figure out what the optimum scan resolution should be when you know exactly what size your scanned image will be for final output. For example, a color 8" x 10" (20.3cm x 25.4cm) image scanned at 100 percent using a 1.5-to-1 sample rate for 133-lpi output (200 spi) results in a more manageable 9.6MB file. When printed at the same size, the quality of this 200-spi image is more than adequate for most printing applications.

FPO SAMPLING These are low-resolution images used for position only that will be replaced with a much higher resolution version of the same image at a later time. They require a minimum amount of memory, meaning they are faster to work with and easier to store than high-resolution images. A typical sample rate is 72 spi, which matches most screen resolutions. A color 8" x 10" (20.3cm x 25.4cm) image scanned at 72 spi results in a mere 1.2MB (24-bit color) or 414K (8-bit color) file size.

Step 5: Adjust Tone Controls

Your tone controls depend on your particular software/hardware combination. The names for the various tone controls and how they perform are not consistent from program to program. For example, some programs use the term *lightness* for gamma (midtone lightness), whereas others use gamma for overall lightness. Unfortunately, you can only determine how to adjust tone controls on your scanner by reading and understanding your user's manual or calling the manufacturer's technical help line.

Bit Depth, Scan Mode and File Size

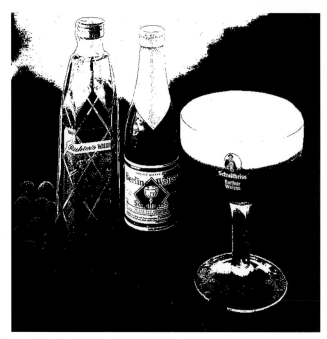

This 1-bit dithered image has a file size of 64K.

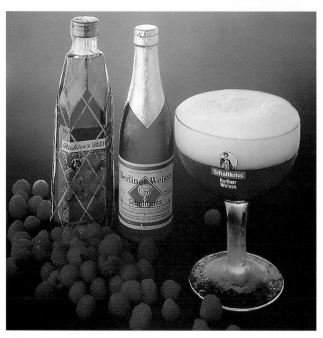

This 8-bit grayscale image, with 256 shades of gray, has a file size of 518K.

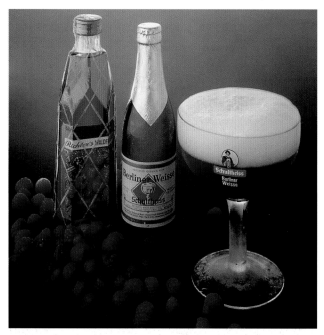

This 8-bit color image, with 256 colors, has a file size of 518K.

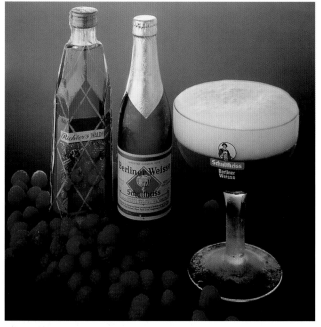

This 24-bit color image, with 26 million colors, has a file size of 1.55MB.

Typical setting choices include:

DMIN/DMAX These are density settings that use a logarithmic scale from 0 to 4, where 0 equals pure white and 4 equals pure black. (Most scanners limit you to about 0.1 Dmin to 3.2 Dmax.) Choose the maximum density (Dmax) and the minimum density (Dmin) for the data in your image to map to. This setting is similar to Set White Point/Set Black Point, described below, except it allows you to set controls numerically.

SET WHITE POINT/SET BLACK POINT This option lets you choose precisely which samples or portions of the image will map to pure white and pure black. All other colors will fall between these two extremes. A nice feature that comes with some applications allows you to remove any color cast in the white/black sample point as well.

SET NEUTRAL POINT OR GRAY BALANCE A very useful tool indeed, if your scanner software supports it. This option allows you to force a specific color to be scanned as neutral (i.e., equal amounts of red, green and blue). The consequence being that the software then adjusts the master input curve for the entire image to achieve the desired result.

EXPOSURE This option is especially useful when working with very dark originals where the scanner may not "see" details in shadowed areas. However, very few scanners actually support this feature. Thus, if you see this option, be suspicious—it might really be just a linearized lightness control, which I recommend avoiding.

LIGHTNESS You should probably avoid using this control if your scanning software offers it unless, of course, this is your scanner manufacturer's terminology for gamma or midtone brightness. Technically, *lightness* is a linearized "curve" that increases overall lightness by cropping out key data in a highlight region of the image. (I'll explain more about linear adjustments later in this chapter.)

CONTRAST You should probably avoid using this control as well. Technically, *contrast* is a linearized "curve" that increases midtone contrast by cropping out key data in the highlight and shadow regions of the image.

GAMMA Gamma is also known as midtone brightness. With 1.0 as the median for an image's midtones, adjusting the gamma to 1.5 lightens the midtones of an image while a gamma setting of 0.75 darkens them.

TONE CURVE Customized tone curve adjustments go beyond simple gamma controls. When you adjust the tone curve of an image you're adjusting the concentration of tone detail. See Using Tone Controls, page 23.

IMPORT TONE CURVE This is probably the most powerful feature for adjusting tones (if your scanning software offers it). Using this option allows you to import a tone curve from an image-editing program that optimizes the way in which the scanner captures the data from an original.

HISTOGRAM This control shows a chart that depicts, on a scale of 1 to 256, the number of instances within an image where one of 256 shades of gray appears. It is a "snapshot" of the distribution of data within your image. Thus, dark (low-key) images have most of the sample points skewed to the left, while light (high-key) images have most of the data samples skewed to the right.

Step 6: Choose Other Options

Some scanner/scanning software combinations offer Sharpening, Descreening and other controls. It is usually more efficient to take advantage of these options at scan time rather than doing them later.

NOTE: For dark originals where there is the likelihood of noise generated by the scanner, it is advisable to selectively sharpen light regions after scanning.

Step 7: Scan

The time involved in scanning depends on the size of the scan (determined by the overall resolution and bit depth), the speed of your scanner, SCSI bus and computer. Scanning used to be fairly time-consuming; however, newer scanners and computers are more than twice as fast as yesterday's models. Even 20MB images may now appear on your screen in a matter of seconds.

NOTE: Many computers today are capable of multitasking, which enables you to perform several functions, such as scan, print, save, use a modem and lay out pages, all at the same time.

Step 8: Save

Do this now, before making any changes! You may want to return to this original.

Optimal Resolution Sizing

This 72-spi image works fine as an FPO image and has a manageable file size.

292K

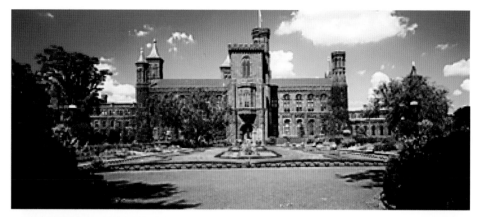

This 150-spi image scanned at a scale of 100 percent from a 5" x 7" chrome yields an image that doesn't hold as much detail as you generally want for output to print.

1.24MB

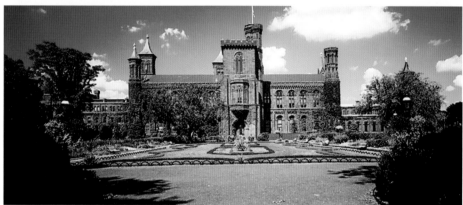

This 225-spi scan was scanned at 100 percent. This combination of scaling and resolution produces this best image for output to print.

2.78MB

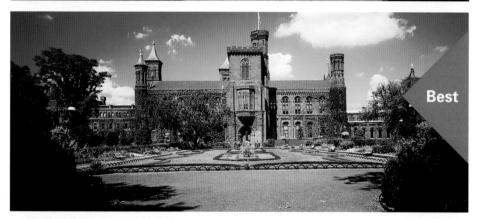

Best

This 300-spi scan was scanned at 100 percent. This combination of scaling and resolution is best when archiving an image.

4.94MB

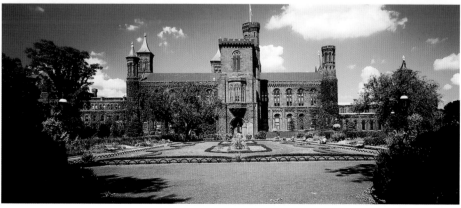

Here are your options:

- Save in proprietary Photoshop native format if you want to work with the image in this program. While Photoshop native format can't be opened by desktop publishing programs, it is run-line encoded (RLE) for compact file size and it offers the ability to save alpha layers, masks and clipping paths with the file.

- Save as a PICT, BMP, GIF or JPEG file if you want to use the image as is for computer display. Many multimedia programs such as Macromedia Director, Apple Media Kit and HyperCard only work with PICT. BMP and PICT images can also be imported as templates for autotracing in illustration programs.

- Save in TIFF or EPS, the most popular file formats for desktop publishing. TIFF images can be imported into page layout programs. EPS files are used when a clipping path and/or CMYK separations are used.

Personally, I prefer to save the original scan in Photoshop format; that way, I know it's the "original." Only after I have scaled the image to its final size and made other adjustments for maximum printability, do I save the image, using a different name, as a TIFF, EPS or PICT file as appropriate.

Step 9: Clean Up Image in an Image-Editing Program

At this stage you should remove dust, eliminate scratches, selectively brighten and/or darken, remove noise, resize, crop further, color correct, soften, sharpen, etc.

NOTE: This work is time-consuming but *very valuable*. You should work at the highest resolution your equipment can handle. Resample your image down to a more convenient (or appropriate) size later.

Step 10: Save Again

Save this image with a different name so, if necessary, you can go back to the original scan at a later date. Of course the downside of saving two images is that you have two versions taking up valuable storage space on your hard disk.

Understanding Tone Curves and Histograms

I know it may seem intimidating, but you need to understand tone curves to produce anything beyond mediocre scans. Even professionals get confused by the complex interfaces found in powerful scanning and image manipulation programs. But don't fret. It's really rather simple.

All image manipulation and scanning tools have one thing in common: They all depict, and thus provide an interface to, the mapping of an input sample to a corresponding output sample. The classic method is a tone curve as shown in figure 1.

An alternative (and complementary) tonal correction method is the histogram. Histograms, as shown in figure 2, depict the distribution of tones within an image. The legend depicts the relationship between each input tone and its corresponding output tone.

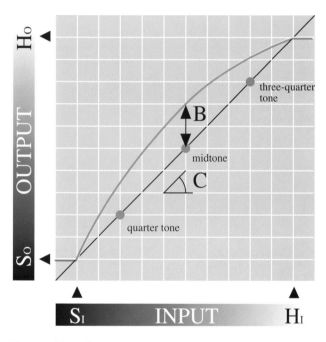

Figure 1: Tone Curve.

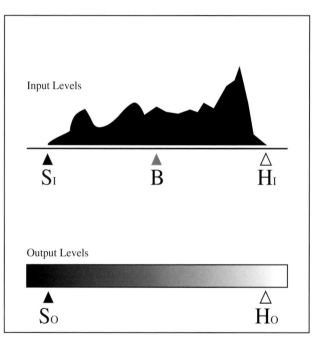

Figure 2: Histogram.

KEY

S_I = Shadow dot (input)
H_I = Highlight dot (input)
B = Midtone brightness
C = Contrast (angle of curve)
S_o = Shadow dot (output)
H_o = Highlight dot (output)

The key thing to remember is that tone curves and histograms do the same thing—map input tones to output tones. The difference is that histograms give you visual feedback, providing information on tone distribution within the image. Unfortunately, histogram adjustment is rare in scanning software; most programs just offer tone controls.

Tone Curves Made Easy

In theory, input should match output one-to-one. But that's theory. In reality, most desktop scanners can't reproduce shadow detail correctly—they simply don't have enough "vision" to see into the darker portions of an image. Thus, most desktop scans lack shadow detail and are generally too dark.

Mastering nonlinear tonal corrections, also known as gamma correction, is really a matter of bringing out the detail in the dark areas of an image and adjusting the tone range to compensate for darkness.

The key to bringing out the detail in the dark portions of an image is in increasing the contrast in that area. The more contrast you have in any given area of an image, the more differentiation there is between shades of gray—resulting in the perception of both more detail and emphasis in that area.

The degree of steepness in a tone curve corresponds to the degree of contrast. But there's a catch—you can't have a steep curve everywhere in an image! Every steep or high contrast area needs to be offset by a shallow or flat area. This is a zero sum game, people.

Likewise, you don't always get the best results if you adjust the tone curve setting on your scanner to a perfectly straight 45° angle, which represents an exact one-to-one mapping. Almost all images need some "help." Some images have important detail in the shadow areas, some have important detail in the highlight region and some have midtone emphasis. Some images are too contrasty, some too flat, some too light, some too dark.

There are two reasons why it's far better to achieve an optimal tone curve at scan time than to manipulate the image later: First, it takes less time to scan an image correctly than to scan it poorly and adjust or manipulate it later. Second, every time you manipulate an image, you lose some data, even if just a bit. The cumulative effect of too many post-scan image manipulations is an image with less data.

Using Tone Controls

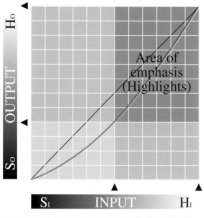

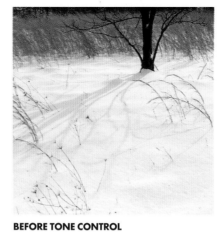

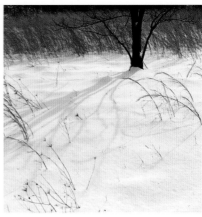

TONE CONTROL FOR SHADOW EMPHASIS   **BEFORE TONE CONTROL**   **AFTER TONE CONTROL**

For high-key originals (mostly lights) you want more contrast in the highlight area. The gamma equals 0.75.

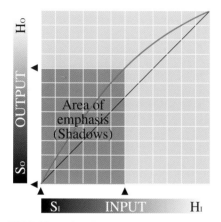

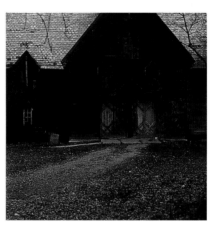

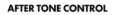

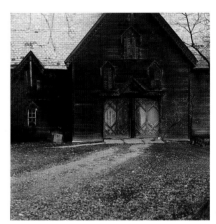

TONE CONTROL FOR HIGHLIGHT EMPHASIS   **BEFORE TONE CONTROL**   **AFTER TONE CONTROL**

For low-key originals (mostly darks) you want more contrast in the shadow area. The gamma equals 1.5.

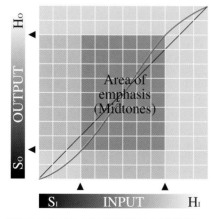

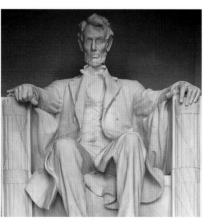

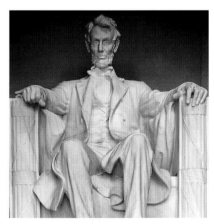

TONE CONTROL FOR MIDTONE EMPHASIS   **BEFORE TONE CONTROL**   **AFTER TONE CONTROL**

For some images you want slightly more contrast in the midtones. This is also known as a classic S-curve.

To achieve the best results, keep the contrast angle steep for the most important areas of the image. There is no one formula that works best for all images. Your understanding of this fact already makes you a much better scanner operator!

Linear Corrections—A Major Post-Scanning Mistake

Fortunately, most scanning applications don't provide brightness and contrast controls, both of which are examples of linear correction. A linear correction, as the name implies, adjusts the default tone "curve" (a straight line) up and down or changes the angle of the line. In the post-scanning environment, using linear corrections is a no-no—you lose important data. More specifically, adjusting brightness shifts the tone line straight up. Data is lost in the highlights and simply disappears.

Contrast adjustments perform in a similar, linear manner. Although detail in the midtone grays is improved, the original input shadow detail is mapped to pure black, resulting in permanent data loss.

See pages 26-27 for an illustration of linear corrections.

Film vs. Paper Output

Paper output halftones are typically limited to about 110 lpi. This is because paper originals must be photographed by the printer in order to make film negatives and then plates for the printing press. When photographing the original, some detail is lost, particularly the small dots in the lighter regions of the image.

Outputting to film eliminates a step because film negatives are used to make the plates. Consequently, very small dots can be used. In general, you should output to film negatives (or film positives for processes such as silkscreen) whenever possible. They give the best results.

Dot Gain — or Spot Variation

Scanning for a computer monitor is easy. A 24-bit monitor can faithfully reproduce every sample in your scanned image. However, if your image looks just right on your computer monitor, it will probably print too dark on press. This is due, in part, to the inability of the four process inks (cyan, magenta, yellow and black) to exactly

FACTORS AFFECTING DOT GAIN

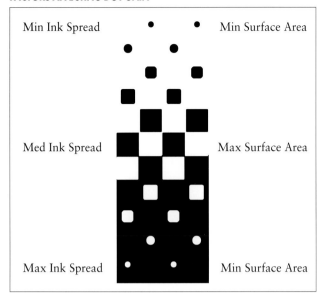

Min Ink Spread — Min Surface Area

Med Ink Spread — Max Surface Area

Max Ink Spread — Min Surface Area

reproduce every color in the spectrum. It's also due to the fact that ink spreads beyond the perimeter of the halftone spot when it is applied to paper, a phenomenon known as dot gain.

The amount of this spread is affected by the absorbency of the paper and the surface area of each individual spot. The porous surface of uncoated paper absorbs much more ink than the smooth surface of a coated paper, causing the ink to spread more, although even the shiniest of coated papers exhibits some dot gain. On an uncoated sheet, the darkest gray or shade of any color you can use without losing detail varies from an 88 percent to 95 percent tint.

Spots with greater surface area tend to exhibit more dot gain. This is especially true in areas with adjacent square halftone spots—ink tends to bridge the gap between spots, creating even greater dot gain. For this reason midtone spots generally spread more than either highlight or shadow spots.

An altogether different problem occurs when printing the lightest tints in an image. You see, a 5 percent spot at 150 lpi is *extremely* small. On press, anything smaller than this will probably not print. The combination of factors involved in offset lithography—water, blankets and offsetting—make it hard for very small dots to hold ink.

The net effect is that an image that looks "right" on your computer monitor (unless your monitor is specially calibrated for offset printing) does not print well on press. Usually, it exhibits loss of detail in shadow regions, highlight regions drop out and midtones are "muddy"—yuck!!

Thus, for printing you should prepare an image so that its maximum and minimum spots are as depicted in the Screen Guidelines for Optimum Halftone Output chart (see page 28). You may also want to set gamma (or midtone lightness) an additional 1.2 to lighten the midtone dot for most presses.

You can specify these tints when you scan if your scanning software supports it. Or you can adjust these settings in an image-editing program such as Photoshop after you scan by using the LEVELS command (see page 21 for more on input and output levels).

What Not to Do: Making Linear Adjustments

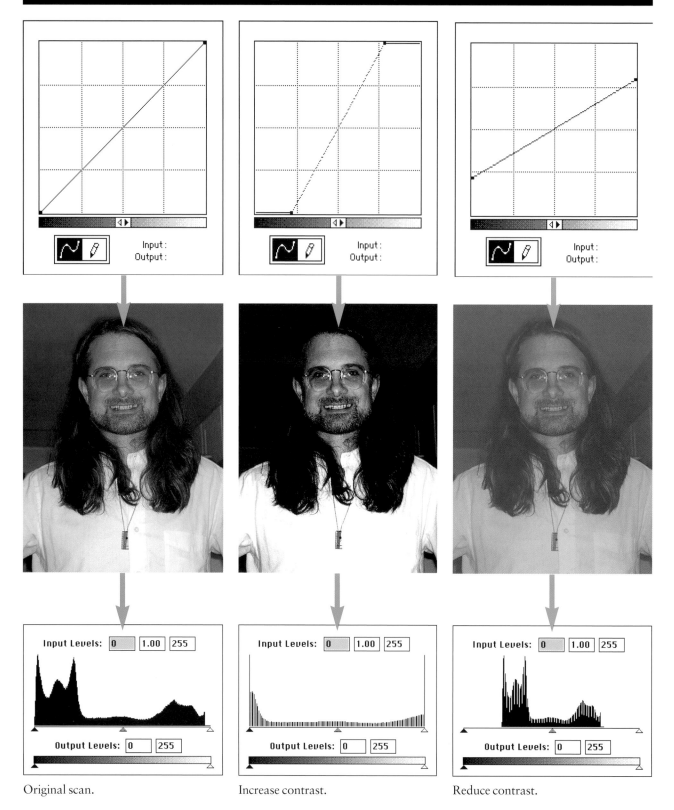

Original scan.

Increase contrast.

Reduce contrast.

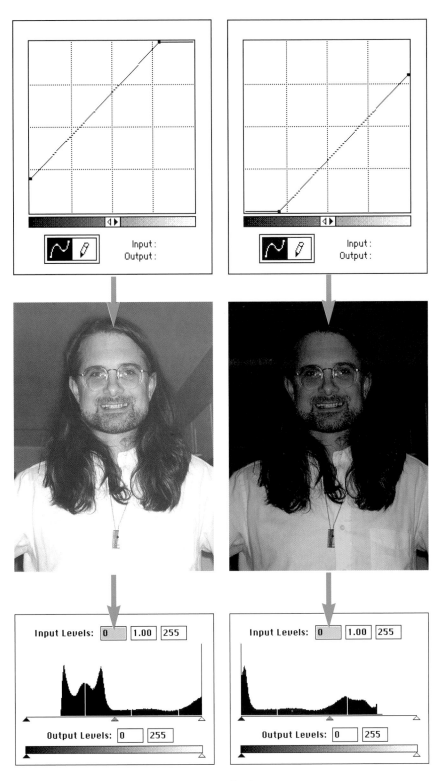

Input :
Output :

Input :
Output :

Input Levels: 0   1.00   255

Input Levels: 0   1.00   255

Output Levels: 0   255

Output Levels: 0   255

Lighten.

Darken.

Screen Guidelines for Optimum Halftone Output

PAPER	MINIMUM TINT	MAXIMUM TINT	MIN OUTPUT LEVEL (on a scale of 0-256 in Photoshop's LEVELS dialog)	MAX OUTPUT LEVEL
Coated	5%	95%	12	243
Uncoated	10%	90%	25	230
Newsprint	12%	88%	30	225

Simply open the LEVELS dialog box (Command-L in Photoshop), type in the appropriate numbers for shadow output (S_O), highlight output (H_O) and midtone lightness (B) (consult Screen Guidelines for Optimum Halftone Output). Click OK and save as a new file name. The image on your screen may look somewhat washed out, but rest assured, it will give you optimum results on press.

I prefer to scan at full tonal range, since much of my scanning work is also used for multimedia purposes. Then, when I go to print, I modify the image file as appropriate for the intended output/paper combination and dot gain. I then save the modified image with a new file name. This way I have two versions of the image: the "screen" or master version that looks just the way I want it to look and the "print" version.

NOTE: Some color separation software is now able to perform dot gain on the fly at imagesetting time—check with your service bureau to see if they can provide this service for you.

How Paper Affects an Image

As mentioned earlier, the quality of an image is affected by the type of paper on which it is printed. Your paper choice dictates the maximum printing screen frequency (lpi) you can achieve, and the lpi you select affects the spi setting to use for your image file.

In general, use an spi setting from 1.41 to 2 times the printing screen frequency (lpi). Low-resolution scans should be used for 300-dpi laser output where more data won't improve the resolution of an image. On the other hand, high-resolution offset printing on coated stock demands a scan at a much higher spi setting, resulting in a correspondingly larger file.

For more information on additional sources explaining dot gain, prepress issues and printing standards see page 133 in chapter five.

The Best Screen Frequencies by Output

PRINTING METHOD	PAPER USED	SCREEN FREQUENCY	SCAN @ 1.5 TO 1
Xerographic copier	Laser paper	50-75 lpi	75-125 spi
Quick print (paper plates)	Uncoated	50-75 lpi	75-125 spi
	Coated	75-110 lpi	125-175 spi
Offset lithography	Uncoated	85-133 lpi	125-200 spi
	Coated	120-175 lpi	180-300 spi

File Size and Storage

Needless to say, scanning images takes lots of hard disk space. And unless you have terabytes of free space, sooner or later you have to deal with where to put all this neat stuff.

I prefer to scan at the highest resolution first, manipulate the image to remove dust and scratches, do some minor color correcting, and archive the (large) file to Zip, Jaz or DAT backup. I then make an optimally sized image for my intended use by resizing down. At this time I apply sharpening and any other image manipulation as necessary. All this takes place on a (mostly) clean 4.0GB fast hard disk.

Nevertheless, I often find myself swamped with hundreds of megabytes of images in no time flat. For this reason I prefer 100MB Zip and 1.0GB Jaz drives. I have one disk for each of my clients and their respective projects. Occasionally, I need one drive for just one project! Even then, I make DAT backups of the whole enchilada, in case I lose or damage my Zip drives.

It goes without saying that you also need a large hard disk to work on your active projects. Photoshop not only works best with a lot of RAM but also needs a lot of free hard disk space. Therefore, it's important to keep your main hard disk clean most of the time. Backing up your files on a daily basis (weekly at the very least) is of utmost importance.

I have outlined a few of the more popular large storage media available. Unfortunately, prices change monthly. Use this chart as a rough comparison only. But remember, you should choose media that will be compatible with others as well. Call your service bureaus or other vendors and ask them what they use. Most people will gladly give you their opinions (just take it with a grain of salt!).

Storage Media: Find the Best Option for Your Needs

TYPE	SIZE	DRIVE COST	MEDIA COST	ACCESS TIME	THROUGHPUT
SyQuest	88MB	$300	$30	30ms	1MB/sec
	Remarks: Compatible with SyQuest 44 Low cost for drives, high cost per megabyte for media				
SyQuest	200MB	$800	$60	30ms	1MB/sec
	Remarks: Compatible with SyQuest 44 and 88 Low cost for drives, high cost per megabyte for media				
SyQuest EZ	135MB	$299	$20	15ms	17MB/sec
	Remarks: Not quite as universal as other SyQuest types Competitor to the more popular Iomega Zip drive				
SyQuest SyJet	1.5GB	$599	$100	10-12ms	5.4MB/sec
	Remarks: Inexpensive solution for storage, low cost per megabyte Competitor to the Iomega Jaz drive				
Hard disks	2.0GB+	$399+	NA	8ms	4.3MB/sec
	Remarks: Needs backup to be safe SCSI-2 RAID drives can be two to four times as fast as listed here				
Magneto Optical	128MB	$900	$20	40ms	700KB/sec
	Remarks: Slow writes, fast reads Compact 3.5" media High cost for drives, low cost per megabyte for media				
Magneto Optical	4.6GB	$1,700	$225	21ms	3.5MB/sec
	Remarks: Slow writes, fast reads Great for large multimedia or design projects Manufactured by Apex				
CD recordable	650MB	$1,000	$10	200ms	300KB/sec
	Remarks: Very slow writes and throughput High cost for drives, low cost per megabyte for media				
DAT	1-2GB	$700	$20	varies (depends on where file is on tape)	
	Remarks: Requires backup software to access files Lowest cost per megabyte for media				
DAT	4-8GB	$1,000	$20	varies (depends on where file is on tape)	
	Remarks: Requires backup software to access files Lowest cost per megabyte for media				
Iomega Zip Drive	100MB	$199	$20	29ms	1.40MB/sec
	Remarks: Inexpensive solution for storage Very popular				
Iomega Jaz Drive	1GB	$599	$99	10-12ms	5.4MB/sec
	Remarks: Inexpensive solution for storage Low cost per megabyte				

CHAPTER TWO

Types of Scans and Scanners

How to Buy a Scanner

Buying a scanner may seem simple enough. A scanner is a scanner, you might think. But buying the right scanner is a bit like buying a car—you don't want to get stuck with something you'll regret later.

There are a wide variety of scanner types to choose from with a broad range of capabilities and uses. Although flatbed scanners are by far the most popular type, other types of scanners have their places and should not be dismissed. Depending on the type of work you do, two (or more) different types of scanners may be appropriate. In my own design office, we use a flatbed, a slide scanner, a video digitizer, a digitizing tablet and Photo CD—frequently using all of them on the same project.

How Fast a Scanner?

One thing to consider when scanning an image is how long it takes to scan a file that needs color correcting. I'm not talking about the raw speed of getting a single image into your computer, but rather the overall time it takes to correct/adjust an image and then scan. Speedy scanners with old-fashioned software are as inefficient as slow scanners with more up-to-date scanning software. Unfortunately, many manufacturers are doing just that—taking old scanner designs and selling them with new, improved software. Conversely, other manufacturers are shipping newer scanner mechanisms with old-style software. Neither is optimal.

The ideal scanning setup provides fast, noise-free scans and allows you to interactively change tone, contrast and color controls during the preview mode. Once you see what you're looking for in preview mode, you should be able to simply select, scan and presto—the image you want (with no further need for color correcting) is in your computer. Scanning software that forces you to scan once, correct in Photoshop, then rescan is old-fashioned and, ultimately, less productive, regardless of the stated speed of the machine.

Consider the Individual Components

Scanners are complex systems that differ markedly in the quality they produce. Like a cheap stereo, a low-end scanner is OK for "background" music but not necessarily for achieving high fidelity. In general, you get what you pay for.

Likewise, the quality of each component affects the final result—after all, a chain is

Component Rater

SCANNER FEATURE OR COMPONENT	BEST FLATBED SCANNERS	ENTRY-LEVEL FLATBED SCANNERS
Lightsource	Cold-cathode	Fluorescent
Optics	Color-corrected coated prisms	Plastic
# of sensors	Multiple CCD array	Single CCD array
Sensor resolution	5,000-8,000	3,000-4,000
Sample density per scan line	600-1,000 spi	300-400 spi
Sample density per step	1,200-2,000 spi	600-800 spi
Bit per sample	10 -14 bit	8 bit
Dynamic range	3.0-3.3	2.2-2.9
Analog-to-digital converter	High-end, electrically isolated	Low-end, integrated
Box design	Sealed case	Open case

When shopping for a scanner, use this chart to evaluate each component.

only as strong as its weakest link. The table above lists the various features common to all flatbed scanners and lists which options provide the best quality.

Wanting It All: High Resolution and Dynamic Range

When evaluating a flatbed scanner, two of the most important features to consider are its resolution and its dynamic range. Ideally, you want both high resolution and high dynamic range. In practice, it is hard to achieve. Here's why.

Most desktop scanners, including transparency and flatbed, use linear CCD (charge-coupled device) array technology. Linear CCD arrays are similar to the CCD panels used in video cameras except they are arranged in a single array rather than a matrix so they can capture an individual line or "scan" of data at a time.

The vast majority of scanners on the market use a linear array of 2,000, 3,000, 4,000, 5,000, 6,000 or even 8,000 CCDs. By using CCDs, desktop scanners can be small and inexpensive to produce. However, CCD technology is limited in the degree of resolution it can achieve. For example, a scanner using a 5,000-array CCD scanning an 8.3" (21cm) original can produce, at most, a 600-spi scan. Scanner manufacturers make up for this limitation by "stepping" the CCD array at a much higher frequency, for example, 1,200 spi. Each square inch of data is made up of, at most, 600 x 1,200 samples. Most scanning software interpolates this data to achieve an effective resolution of 1,200 x 1,200 samples, but this is not the same as a true (optical)

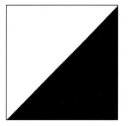

Original artwork.

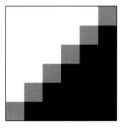

600 x 600 spi.

600 x 1,200 optical interpolated to 1,200 x 1,200 spi.

600 x 600 optical interpolated to 1,200 x 1,200 spi.

1,200 x 1,200 optical.

1,200 x 1,200-spi scan. In fact, all else being equal, a typical 600 x 1,200 scanner is only marginally better than a 600 x 600 scanner.

Dynamic range is the total amount of optical density deliverable by a scanner. In effect, it describes the darkest shadow you can achieve. Similar to the Richter scale used to measure earthquakes, dynamic range is measured using a logarithmic scale on which 0 equals pure white (also known as Dmin) and 4.0 equals pure black (also known as Dmax). The higher your dynamic range the better, because each increase in numerical value represents ten times more potential data. A scanner that delivers a dynamic range of 3.2 is ten times "better" than one that delivers a dynamic range of 2.2!

Unfortunately, the ability of an individual CCD to capture the dynamic range of an image sample is directly related to its size. In general, the larger the CCD, the better its dynamic range. But for a flatbed, where the number of CCD elements in an array determines the final number of samples per inch, the larger the size of the CCD elements, the smaller the available resolution. Alternatively, if you increase the number of CCDs in the array, the dynamic range suffers because the size of the CCD itself, by necessity, gets smaller. It's a catch-22!

Most entry-level flatbed scanners have a dynamic range from 2.2 to 2.9. Midlevel flatbed scanners deliver a dynamic range from 3.0 to 3.2. High-level drum scanners can achieve a dynamic range all the way up to 4.0 (they use different technology). While a dynamic range of 4.0 may be desirable, achieving it may be moot—nothing you can scan actually has a 4.0 dynamic range. Typical reflected art maxes out at a dynamic range of 2.3, while the most a properly exposed 4" x 5" (10.2cm x 12.7cm)

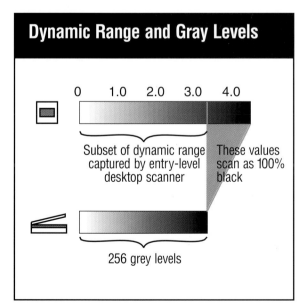

Theoretical dynamic range and how it maps to a flatbed scanner.

transparency can hope to achieve is 3.3 dynamic range. Thus, a scanner with a *noise-free* dynamic range of 3.0 to 3.3 is all you will ever need.

Take a Test Drive

When purchasing a scanner, the biggest factor to take into consideration is how much noise it generates. To test for noise, insist on "test-driving" a scanner before you buy it. Take an image with you that has a good range of shadows, midtones and highlights (in short, your average image). Scan it, bring it into Photoshop, then apply the Equalize command (Image/Adjust/Equalize). If the scanner is of reasonable quality, you won't see any streaks, splotches or bizarre noise in the image (see examples below).

On the other hand, if the scanner is of questionable quality, the Equalize command will bring out and amplify problems in the scan. You should see the look on salespeople's faces when they try to sell me a scanner at a trade show and I pull the "Equalize trick" on them. I've uncovered expensive scanners that are full of flaws using this technique. Likewise, I've found some reasonably priced scanners that provide excellent quality.

THE SCANNER "TEST DRIVE"

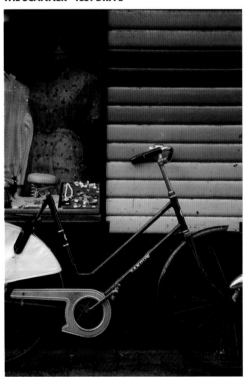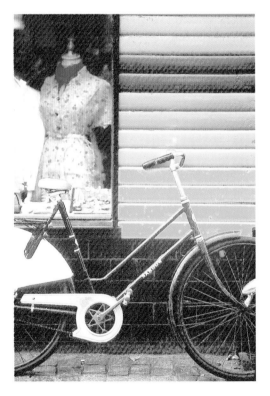

Normal scan.

RIGHT
The same scan after equalization shows heavy banding in the shadows. This scanner has serious problems.

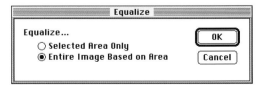

Find a Scanner With a Minimum of Noise

Noise is something all CCD-equipped scanners exhibit to some degree—some more than others. Noise is basically "junk" data. It shows up as random, multicolored sample points introduced into a scan as the result of an engineering fact of life exhibited by all CCD scanners: CCDs produce a very weak signal when digitizing shadow data, and any distortion in the signal introduced by the electronics or motorized mechanism is greatly amplified. This is why you notice it most in the shadow regions of an image. Unfortunately, there are many dark originals out there, and noisy scanners won't do them justice.

Since noise is most affected by the electronic mechanisms that run the scanner, we want to beware of low-end analog-to-digital converters, common to most entry-level scanners, that may introduce noise into the data stream much as a low-fidelity stereo adds hiss and distortion to the playback of fine music. Midlevel scanners isolate the analog-to-digital electronics from the scanner electronics to keep artificially introduced noise to a minimum. The lessons learned by the audio industry are now being adopted by the scanning industry.

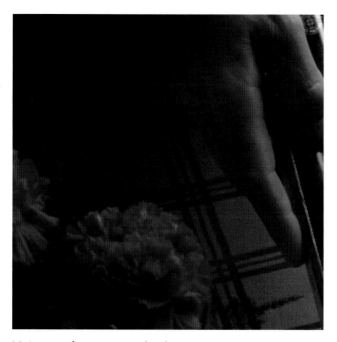

Noisy scan from an entry-level scanner.

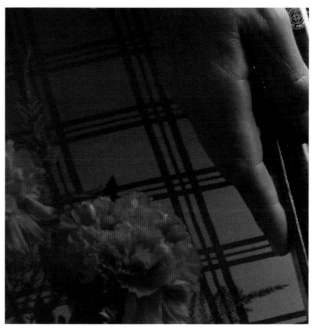

Noise-free scan from a midlevel scanner.

Proper Setup

Installing a scanner is usually quite easy. For the most part it's plug and play. That is, you plug your scanner into your computer, install the scanner software and play! But there can be a few "gotchas" along the way.

Some scanners have proprietary interface cards—these should be avoided, if possible, unless you (a) are getting an incredible deal, (b) prefer that particular kind of interface or (c) get masochistic pleasure from fiddling with your computer and resolving any incompatibilities that may ensue.

A better alternative is to choose a scanner with an SCSI interface. The big advantage to SCSI is that you can easily add on a variety of devices, everything from CD-ROM drives to removable hard disks, tape drives, modems and, of course, other scanners.

Most scanners are now available in SCSI versions—and for good reason: SCSI is an open, fast and generally reliable technology. However, many scanner communication problems are caused by borderline SCSI subsystems. You may have a borderline SCSI system if you have experienced any of the following: scans that fail to finish, slow performance, "can't find scanner" warnings or mysterious program crashes and errors. Even hard disk crashes can be traced to failures or conflicts somewhere in the SCSI chain. Some people never have SCSI problems and can't understand what all the fuss is about. Others curse their computers daily and wonder what they did wrong in a previous life.

For PC users an SCSI driver needs to be loaded into your CONFIG.SYS file. Typically, this file is tagged with a name such as ASPI.SYS, which stands for Advanced SCSI Programming Interface. Mac users have it easy—SCSI has been a Mac standard since the Mac Plus.

SCSI Gremlins

Unfortunately, even for Mac users, SCSI can be a black art. Master SCSI and you can legitimately call yourself a master of the universe (if you can't master it, don't fret—almost everybody else is in SCSI purgatory as well). But there is salvation. Over the years the tao of SCSI has been revealed to me. Hence, I hereby divulge the Ten SCSI Commandments:

I.   Thou shalt not use cheap SCSI cables.

II.   Thou shalt not use total SCSI cable length greater than eighteen feet.

III.   Thou shalt keep thy SCSI IDs separate.

IV.   Thou shalt use up-to-date hard disk (and CD-ROM) drivers.

V.   Thou shalt consider buying active SCSI termination (such as SCSI Sentry from APS Technologies).

VI.   Thou shalt always use only one terminator at the end of the SCSI chain.

VII.   Thou shalt use similar quality and length cables for all thy SCSI devices.

VIII. Thou shalt patiently wait the coming of new technologies.

IX.   Thou shalt suspect older SCSI hard drives as potential sources of evil.

X.   Thou shalt not attempt to install more than six SCSI devices in one SCSI chain.

Follow the above commandments and you will surely avoid SCSI hell. Disregard them at your peril. Look forward to the coming of FireWire technology from Apple as well as the competing SCSI-3 specification that, eventually, will replace today's SCSI standard entirely. Until then, keep praying.

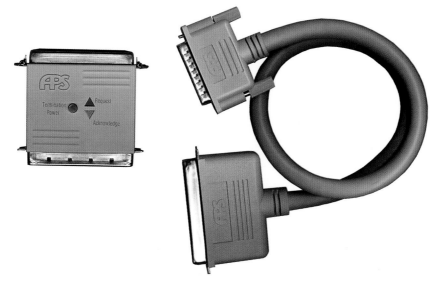

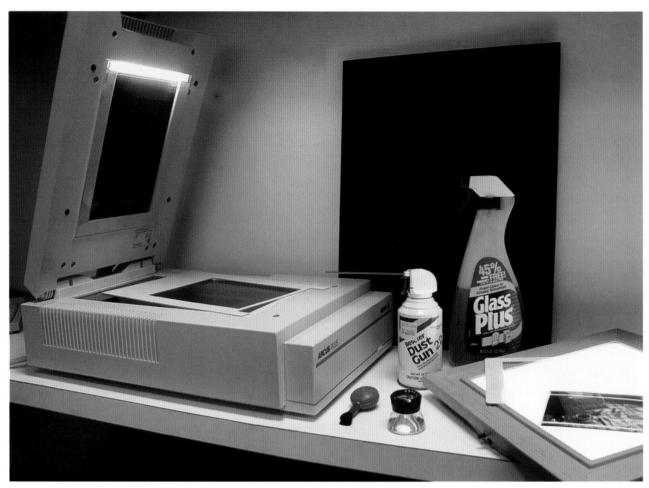

Basic tools: A can of compressed air, glass cleaner, lens brush, black paper, spare scanner bulb, screw drivers, and black paper masks for 2¼" and 4"x 5" transparencies and negatives.

Taking Care of Your Equipment

Most desktop scanners will provide years of trouble-free service—with the possible exception of the lightbulb burning out. Newer designs use cold-cathode tubes that can have lifetimes of 25,000+ hours and, thus, "never" need replacing.

As for most electrical equipment, it is also wise to provide a voltage spike protector. Other than that, the only other thing you need to do for your scanner is clean it, and cleanliness is, indeed, next to godliness. The last thing you want to do after obtaining a quality scan is to manually eliminate unnecessary dust and "grunge" spots.

Placing unusual items on your scanner may be creative, but it also puts your scanner at risk. When scanning "unusual" stuff, keep these points in mind:

- Always clean the glass platen after scanning anything that may have left residue or debris (tape, food, leaves).

- Never put anything with a sharp edge (diamonds, machined objects, hara-kiri swords) on the glass platen—it might make a permanent scratch. Instead, first put down a clear sheet of plastic film; if that gets scratched it won't matter. It's better to be safe than sorry!

- If you work with liquids, don't let any moisture get inside your unit—unless, of course, you actually like buying new equipment.

- Take care with heavy objects! Your scanner would surely object to a sumo wrestler sitting atop it. Be just as careful with heavy books and slabs of marble, too.

- Don't force the cover shut—it may just decide to snap. Instead, cover a bulky object with a white sheet. Some scanning software needs a white background behind a scanned object. On the other hand, you may not need anything at all—give it a try.

Types of Scanners

Flatbed

The most popular type of desktop scanner is the ubiquitous flatbed scanner, so called because of its flat glass platen (or bed) that serves as both the scanning area and the surface for laying down objects to be scanned. Most flatbed scanners are used for scanning reflective art.

Flatbeds can be accessorized to scan transparent originals. In fact, transparency adapters are especially useful for scanning large transparencies, such as 4" x 5" chromes, medical X-rays and 2 ¼" negatives. Flatbed scanners don't offer the high scanning resolution needed for the small 35mm format; dedicated slide scanners produce better scans of slides and color negatives.

A document feeder is another useful flatbed accessory, particularly when scanning for OCR. If you are scanning a book or lengthy document, a document feeder could pay for itself in one project because it allows many pages to be scanned without operator intervention. Not all scanner manufacturers offer document feeders. See chapter five for a list of current products.

If either of the above options will be important to you at a later date, be sure your scanner manufacturer allows you to purchase and install these accessories by yourself. Otherwise, you may have to send the unit back to be outfitted by the manufacturer.

Also make sure your scanning software supports these features. For example, some third-party software won't support either transparency adapters or document feeders. Flatbeds come in three types: entry-level, midlevel and high-end.

ENTRY-LEVEL flatbed scanners generally share the following specifications: 8.3" x 11" (21.0cm x 27.9cm) scanning area, 300- to 600-spi scanning ability (often advertised as interpolated to 800, 1,200 or 1,600 "spi"), 8 bits per color channel and low cost. They often come bundled with "value-added" software such as Adobe PhotoDeluxe. These machines frequently offer an excellent price-to-performance ratio. Because there is fierce competition for this market, at the time of this writing the magic price for entry-level scanners seems to be hovering around the $400 mark.

Entry-level scanners are adequate for capturing line art, for optical character recognition and for FPO (for-position-only) scanning. For professional-looking color output, you may want to consider at least a midlevel scanner.

MIDLEVEL flatbed scanners differ from their entry-level cousins in two important ways: First, they cost much more! Second, they have significantly better specifications. For example, a typical midlevel flatbed scans at 600 x 1,200 spi and 12 bits per color, resulting in scans of significantly higher quality. Some midlevel scanners may also offer a larger scanning area. They typically run from $2,000 to $5,000.

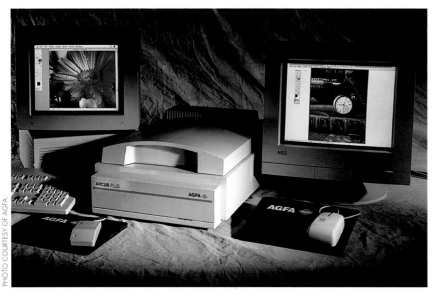

PHOTO COURTESY OF AGFA

Midlevel flatbed scanner.

HIGH-END flatbed scanners are positioned as alternatives to drum scanners. They offer features that professionals demand: noise-free design, large scanning area, high dynamic range and high resolution. Expect to pay a premium price of $6,000 to $20,000 for these scanners. Midlevel scanners are increasingly taking over this territory. Expect the lines to blur between midlevel and high-end flatbeds in the near future.

Transparency Scanners

Transparency scanners come in two versions: multiformat and 35mm.

MULTIFORMAT transparency scanners allow you to scan everything from 35mm slides all the way up to 4" x 5" transparencies. These scanners are targeted to professionals only and thus cost quite a bit, as much as $15,000. In fact, these high-end transparency scanners are muscling in on the once exclusive domain of drum scanners by offering more features, better software and faster scanning time.

35MM transparency scanners, also known as slide scanners, are used to capture both 35mm slides and negatives. Generally, negatives come in strips of film while slides are mounted in cardboard sleeves. Most slide scanners allow you to scan both types. While slide scanners used to be priced for professionals only, recent models introduced by Nikon, Microtek and Polaroid are targeting a broader market. Newer models even offer 12-bit scanning for under $2,000. On the high end, models such as Leafscan 35 and Nikon's LS-3510 generic "base" unit offer 12- and 14-bit scanning, autofocus and advanced scanning software not found on the lower-price models.

Most transparency scanners are, by definition, midlevel devices. Dedicated to scanning transparencies and negatives, they differ from flatbed transparency adapters in several important ways:

- They offer significantly higher scanning frequencies—usually on the order of 1,850 to 4,000 samples for the width of a 35mm slide (whose dimensions are 24mm x 36mm). This translates into a sampling frequency of 1,300 to 2,822 spi.

- They offer superior software algorithms for capturing the subtle differences

SLIDE VS. FLATBED
As you can see from this comparison, dedicated slide scanners can discern differences in film types and are able to compensate for film differences to achieve the best quality.

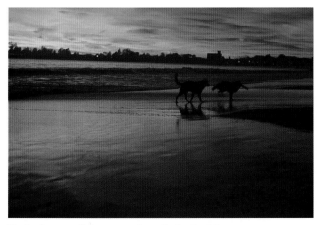

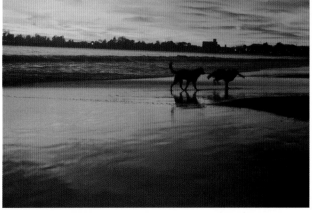

Kodachrome slide scanned on flatbed with transparency option.

Kodachrome slide scanned with dedicated slide scanner.

between different transparency types and color negatives. Because film companies such as Kodak and Fuji manufacture their films differently for consumer and professional use, this can be a significant feature. Your sunsets look great when shooting Kodachrome because "amateur" films like Kodachrome and Fujichrome are oversaturated to give "truer" reds and greens. Ironically, Kodak's and Fuji's professional E6 films are nearly indistinguishable—they don't want to unduly influence a professional photographer's results. Dedicated slide scanners have to know how to distinguish between these two film types. As a result, most transparency scanners come with a fairly complete list of different film types that the scanner software supports and can thus compensate for when scanning.

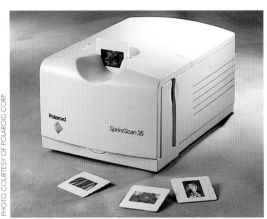

PHOTO COURTESY OF POLAROID CORP.

Slide scanner.

• Slide scanners cost a lot more than the relatively inexpensive flatbed transparency option. For those who may need only an occasional transparency scanned, a flatbed with transparency adapter is the way to go. But if you scan a lot of transparencies, only dedicated transparency scanners offer the best quality scans.

Video Digitizers

Today, most people use video digitizers for multimedia purposes, especially in the creation of QuickTime movies. But that shouldn't prevent you from occasionally using them to capture still images for print.

Video cameras utilize the same digital CCDs found in flatbed scanners. The difference is that video cameras use CCD matrices instead of arrays and can capture an entire image at once, without scanning line by line. Video cameras produce an analog signal that drives other analog devices such as VCRs and television sets. Although video cameras technically aren't "scanners" in the truly digital sense of the word, the analog video signal can be redigitized using specialized hardware and software in your computer. Video-capture software is very similar to traditional scanning

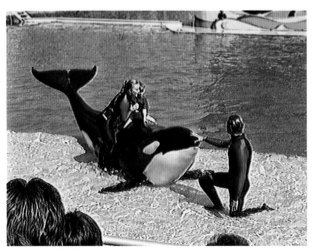

Video capture at 640 x 480 pixels.

software, while the hardware is usually a board that fits inside your computer.

Although video cameras provide an inexpensive way to get images into your computer, you should be aware that the resolution is low (only 640 x 480 pixels) and the dynamic range is low (usually less than 2.5). The color accuracy is also suspect. Nevertheless, video cameras are more than competent—in fact, I've been using them for image capture in my own work since 1987.

Stand-Alone Oversize Digitizers

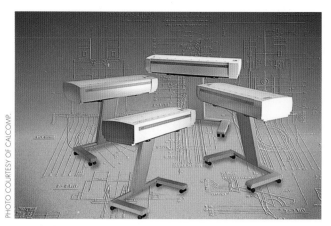

PHOTO COURTESY OF CALCOMP.

Stand-alone digitizer.

For very large originals up to 40" (101.6cm) wide (such as architectural/engineering drawings), several manufacturers offer oversize, sheet-fed digitizers. These unusual devices are somewhat related to the automatic document feeders for flatbed scanners in that the original is pulled through the scanning mechanism. They differ in that the scanner head is stationary; in fact, they often bear a striking resemblance to CAD pen plotters. Because of the large image area involved, and subsequent large file size, sheet-fed digitizers usually can scan only in line art and grayscale modes. Because of their uniqueness and specialization, these devices are also quite expensive, ranging from $10,000 to $20,000 or more.

Miscellaneous

- A pocket-sized device from Trio Information Systems allows you to convert any fax machine into a 1-bit scanner or printer using a standard fax modem and proprietary Trio software. While certainly not high end, such a device may be particularly useful for those using laptops and portables on the road.

- Talk about specialized scanning! Pacific Crest Technologies offers a business card scanner (CardGrabber) that does just what its name implies—it is dedicated to those people who need to input and file tons of business cards! Who knows? It may be just for you.

- In a category by itself, Leaf's Lumina camera/scanner is an unusual piece of equipment. Although it appears to be a digital camera, the Lumina is actually a scanner. It uses standard Nikon bayonet lenses, which give it the same flexibility as an ordinary camera. It scans at 2,700 x 3,400 samples and 36 bits deep and can be mounted on a copy stand to scan flat art and books. By attaching a Nikon slide duplicator, the Lumina can scan slides into Photoshop. You can even use it as a studio "camera"; however, flash units won't work with the Lumina since it scans by imaging line by line. At around $5,000, the Lumina may obviate the need to buy both a slide scanner and a flatbed scanner.

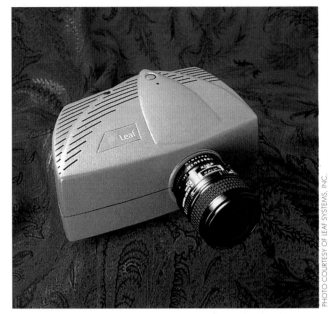

PHOTO COURTESY OF LEAF SYSTEMS, INC.

Camera/scanner.

Photo CD

OK, OK, Photo CD isn't really a type of scanner, but it is a useful way of getting images into your computer. All you need is a CD-ROM drive hooked up to your computer and a roll of film you'd like to look at. Simply send the roll of film out to an authorized Kodak Photo CD developer and for about $1.00 to $3.00 per image you get your film developed along with a CD-ROM containing your digitized images! Pretty neat, huh? Plus CD-ROMs are a great way to keep your image files organized. The quality of these scans is quite good and the proprietary Photo CD format contains several sizes of each individual image for various uses. The largest size, 2,048 x 3,072 samples, is just large enough for a full-bleed 8½" x 11" (21.6cm x 27.9cm) image at 225 spi. It also happens to be the same dimensions as the proposed HDTV (high-definition television) specification—how's that for a coincidence? Pro Photo CD offers even higher resolutions. You can probably get a better scan by using a dedicated slide scanner (see page 43) and not compressing the resulting image. However, if you don't want to buy a slide scanner and learn how to use it, Photo CD may be your best option.

Drum Scanners

Professional color trade shops wouldn't think of using anything less than a drum scanner for producing color separations for high-end printing. Instead of using CCD technology, drum scanners use PMT (photo multiplier tube) technology for greater dynamic range and color accuracy. They also cost an arm and a leg, ranging from $25,000 to $200,000. Nevertheless, drum scanners offer features not available to desktop scanners, such as direct conversion to CMYK, auto sharpening, batch scanning, greater dynamic range and huge image scanning areas. Ironically, most drum scanners don't support preview mode—drum scanner operators are more interested in numbers than what they see with their eyes. Yet what truly sets drum scanners apart is their increased productivity. Since the process of scanning to CMYK is automated, drum scanners can produce more scans per hour than a desktop unit.

Digital Cameras

Digital cameras allow you to shoot three-dimensional objects, much like a regular camera, except you don't have to wait for film developing and processing. Portable units are presently limited in storage and image size. Studio-only units offer larger image size and dynamic range but require attachment to a host computer—hardly a portable solution. In the future, high-resolution, high-quality portable units will surely come—they just aren't here now.

Previous incarnations of "digital" cameras weren't really digital. They digitally sampled the analog signal from a CCD matrix as opposed to converting it to digital data. The resulting data was then stored on floppy disk. The floppy disk then had to be read by a special reader that converted the digital data back into an analog signal, which then had to be redigitized using a video digitizer (see page 44)—what a mess! As you might suspect, the quality wasn't much to write home about, either.

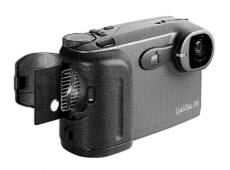

Digital camera.
PHOTO BY JOHN GREENLEIGH, COURTESY OF APPLE COMPUTER, INC.

Newer entry-level digital cameras, such as Apple's QuickTake 200, are truly digital; that is, they keep the signal (nearly) purely digital from the CCD to the floppy disk to the computer. The secret is that they use massive compression of the digital data to get it all to fit on a floppy disk. Typically, these devices save from seven to thirty-two "frames" of digital "frames" of digital data at up to 640 x 480 samples and 24-bit depth. The quality is quite good—good enough for small (2½" x 3½", 6.4cm x 8.9cm) reproductions in print and certainly good enough for many multimedia purposes.

More expensive midlevel digital cameras such as Kodak's DCS 420 use higher resolution CCD panels (1,524 x 1,012 samples) and high-capacity micro hard disks to store the images. The DCS 420 also uses compression to squeeze all that data onto the hard disk. Optional features include digital modems for sending the images back to a "home" office.

High-end digital backs, such as the Dicomed 4000 Big Shot, use even higher resolution CCDs (4,000 x 4,000 or more), higher bit depth (12 bits/sample), higher dynamic range, no compression and high-speed cables connecting the device directly to a computer, where the image is stored and manipulated. Typically, these digital backs attach to a studio camera much as a Polaroid back does. The price of these high-end devices remains in the exclusive domain of professional photographers, and, as you might suspect, the quality is quite good.

Fortunately, the cost of these digital marvels is going down. I predict devices such as these will eventually outsell traditional film cameras—and for good reason: They are convenient, fast, quiet to operate, environmentally friendly and fun to use.

Handheld Scanners

Hand scanners are useful for their portability and low price—often a third to a quarter of the cost of a flatbed scanner. Hand scanners generally plug into a computer's printing port, as opposed to an SCSI port, allowing them to be shared from workstation to workstation. Many people find them ideal for use with a notebook or laptop.

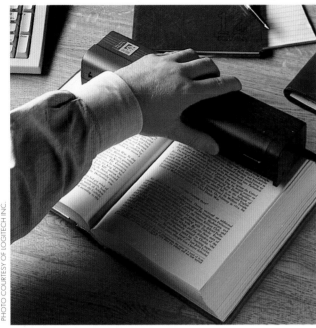

PHOTO COURTESY OF LOGITECH INC.

Handheld scanner.

Unfortunately, hand scanners are less accurate than flatbeds because they have weaker light sources and often produce uneven scans, courtesy of the unsteadiness of your hand or the surface you're standing on. Many hand scanners now offer an alignment template to help guide you when scanning. At least one manufacturer ships a motorized "self-propelled" unit to help stabilize its scanner.

High-end hand scanners offer 400-spi resolution and 24-bit color, allowing you to achieve reasonably high-quality results. But their 4"- to 5"-wide (10.2cm to 12.7cm wide) scan head forces you to make multiple passes to scan even average-size documents. You use the stitching software supplied with these scanners to merge the partial scans together—a time-consuming task. Nonetheless, hand scanners are very popular and are capable of high-quality, quick and easy, low-cost scans.

Scanner Comparison

Take an ordinary 35mm slide. There are many ways to scan it. You could send it out for a drum scan, considered by most to be the best possible method of capturing image data. Or you could send it out for a Kodak Photo CD scan, delivered on a special CD-ROM. But perhaps you were thinking you could do it yourself using your own scanning equipment. Can desktop scanners equal the quality of professionals? I wanted to find out for sure.

I had in my repertoire a three-year-old Agfa Arcus Plus, a newer Epson Expression 636, and a four-year-old Polaroid SprintScan 35, all of which had been advertised as midlevel solutions. I also had the services of a Photo CD lab and a traditional drum scanner available to me. How different would the results be?

Early on I realized that the newer Epson 636, even though it "only" offered 600-spi resolution, gave me better 1,200-spi interpolated scans than my older Agfa Arcus Plus, even though the latter had 600 x 1,200 resolution—a fact that should have favored it immensely. I attribute this to the Epson's 36-bit data capture, which gives it in effect higher "spatial" resolution because it can capture more data. Oh well, I guess it's time to retire my old Agfa! (Note: Although my older Agfa is getting a bit long in the tooth, the newer breed of midlevel Agfas are exceptional scanners.)

No attempt was made to enhance the scans on the following pages—all were converted to CMYK in Photoshop "as is." The only bit of leeway I gave myself at scan time was choosing the white point, black point and gray balance (if the software allowed me to). All large scans were downsampled to 6.8" (17.3cm) wide at 300 spi and sharpened with Unsharp Masking with Amount 120, Radius 2, Threshold 5. All detail images were cropped and saved at their scan frequency, sized (not downsampled) to 2" (5.1cm) square. One other note: All Epson scans, save the color negative, were made with ColorSync enabled (neither Polaroid nor Agfa offers ColorSync compatibility as of this writing). My monitor has been ColorSync-calibrated with a profile created using a Light Source Colortron II, so this gave me a fighting chance to compete with the "big boys" with my ordinary desktop equipment.

The image on the next page is a "tweaked" version of one of the scans on the following pages. It was converted into LAB color space, the "lightness" channel was adjusted for maximum black and minimum white, and it was sharpened with Unsharp Masking using the same formula described above. The "a" channel was blurred with Gaussian Blur, Radius 1, and the green component saturation was increased by 50 percent. The "b" channel was likewise blurred, and both the blue

and yellow components' saturation were also increased. It was then converted to CMYK and saved as a TIFF file.

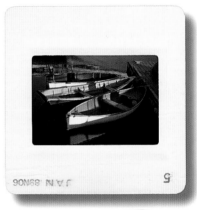

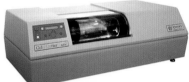

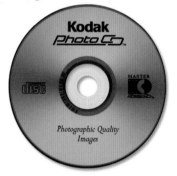

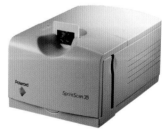

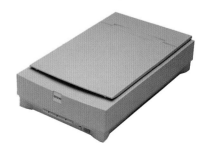

Scanners compared:

MANUFACTURER/ MODEL	PIXEL DEPTH	ADVERTISED RESOLUTION	DENSITY (DMAX)	TYPE OF SCANNER
Agfa Arcus Plus	30 bits	1,200 spi	3.0	Flatbed
Epson Expression 636	36 bits	600 spi	3.0	Flatbed
Polaroid SprintScan 35	30 bits	2,750 spi	3.0	Transparency
Photo CD Pro Scanner	30 bits	4,096 spi	3.2	Flatbed
Optronics Falcon	36 bits	5,400 spi	4.0	Drum

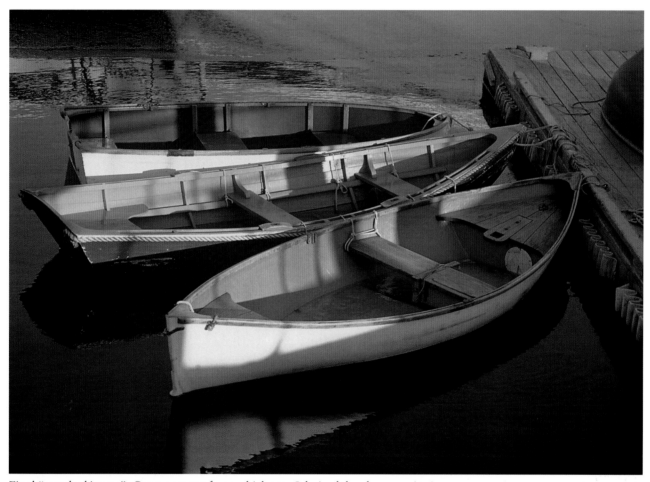

Final "tweaked image". Can you guess from which scan I derived the above version?

Scanner Comparison: Flatbed With Transparency Adapter

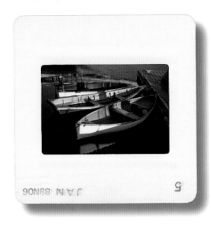

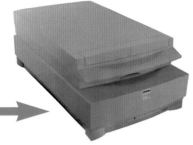

The 35mm slide is scanned on a 36-bit flatbed scanner with transparency adapter at 1,200 spi (interpolated).

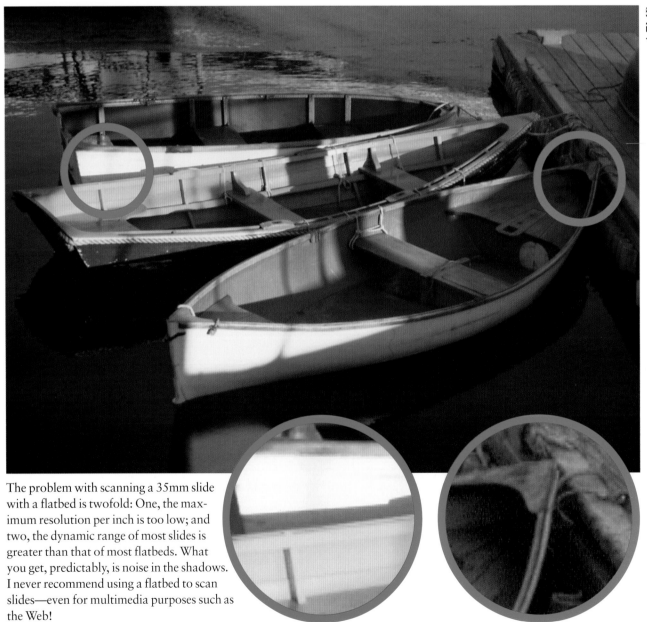

4.7MB

The problem with scanning a 35mm slide with a flatbed is twofold: One, the maximum resolution per inch is too low; and two, the dynamic range of most slides is greater than that of most flatbeds. What you get, predictably, is noise in the shadows. I never recommend using a flatbed to scan slides—even for multimedia purposes such as the Web!

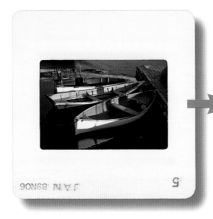

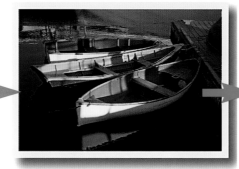

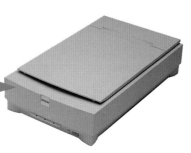

An 8" x 10" (20.3cm x 25.4cm) print is made from a 4" x 5" (10.2cm x 12.7cm) internegative of the original 35mm slide.

It is scanned on a 36-bit flatbed scanner at 300 spi.

15MB

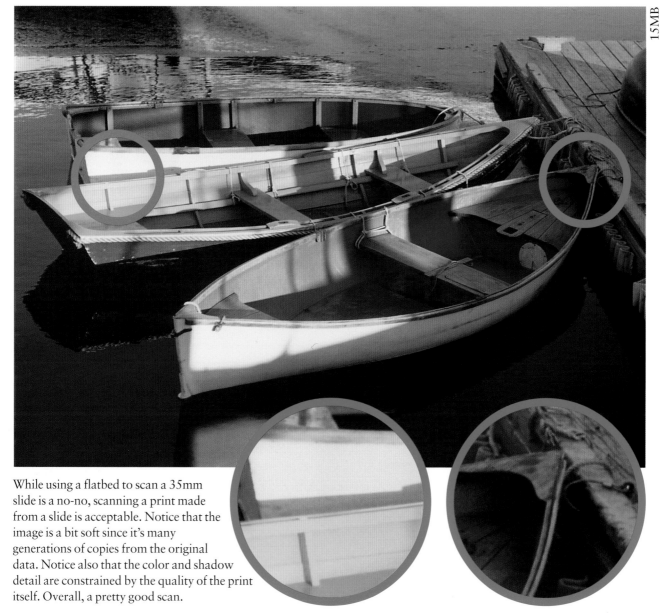

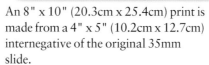

While using a flatbed to scan a 35mm slide is a no-no, scanning a print made from a slide is acceptable. Notice that the image is a bit soft since it's many generations of copies from the original data. Notice also that the color and shadow detail are constrained by the quality of the print itself. Overall, a pretty good scan.

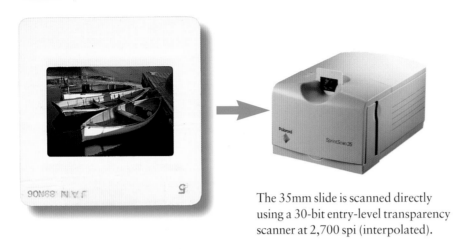

The 35mm slide is scanned directly using a 30-bit entry-level transparency scanner at 2,700 spi (interpolated).

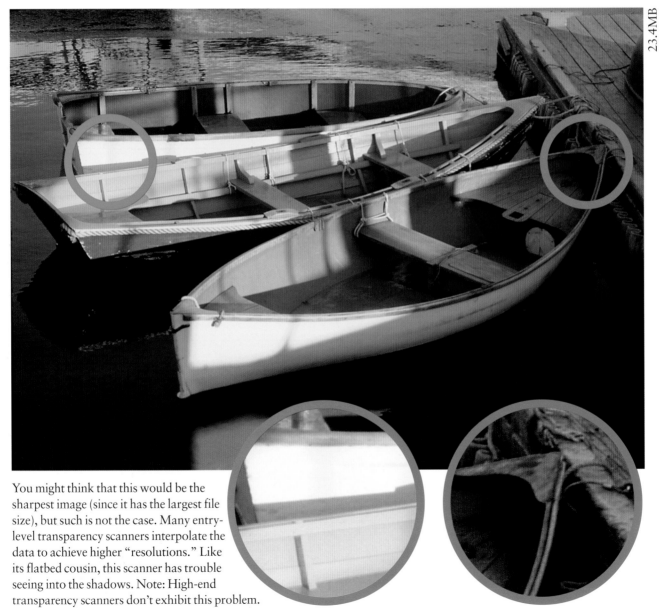

23.4MB

You might think that this would be the sharpest image (since it has the largest file size), but such is not the case. Many entry-level transparency scanners interpolate the data to achieve higher "resolutions." Like its flatbed cousin, this scanner has trouble seeing into the shadows. Note: High-end transparency scanners don't exhibit this problem.

Scanner Comparison: Color Negative

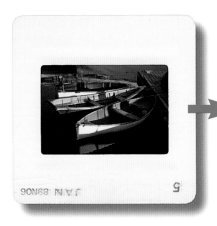 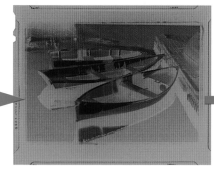 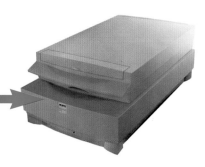

A 4" x 5" (10.2cm x 12.7cm) internegative is made from the original 35mm slide.

It is scanned on a 36-bit flatbed scanner with transparency adapter at 600 spi (optical resolution).

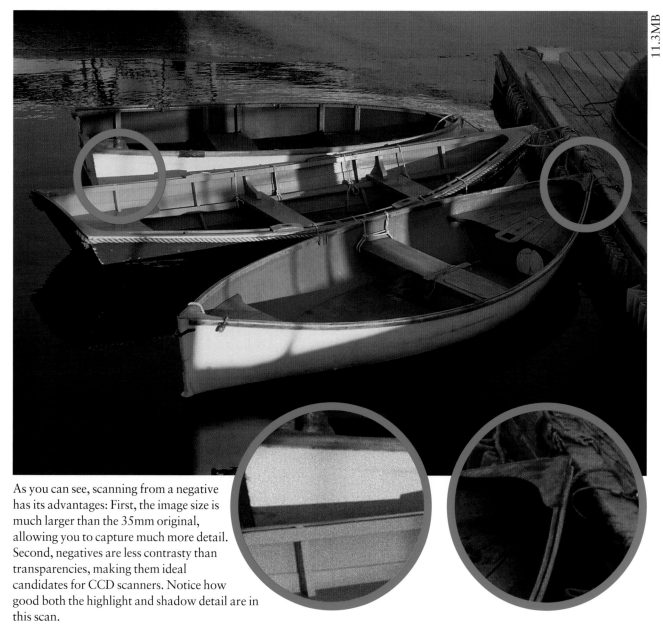

11.3MB

As you can see, scanning from a negative has its advantages: First, the image size is much larger than the 35mm original, allowing you to capture much more detail. Second, negatives are less contrasty than transparencies, making them ideal candidates for CCD scanners. Notice how good both the highlight and shadow detail are in this scan.

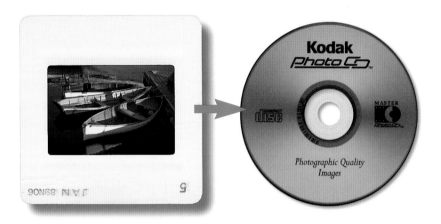

The 35mm slide was scanned to 2,024 x 3,048 samples using Kodak's Pro Photo CD technology. The image was imported directly into Photoshop by specifying Kodachrome as the source and LAB color space as the target. Scan courtesy of Boston Photo, Boston, MA.

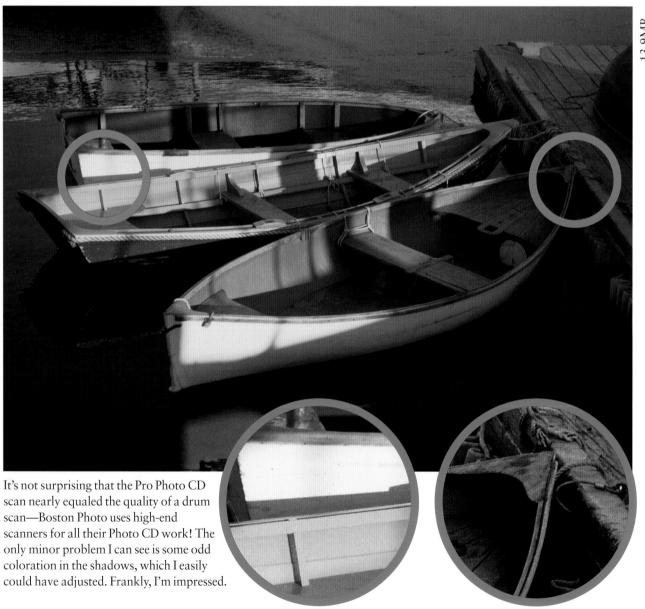

13.9MB

It's not surprising that the Pro Photo CD scan nearly equaled the quality of a drum scan—Boston Photo uses high-end scanners for all their Photo CD work! The only minor problem I can see is some odd coloration in the shadows, which I easily could have adjusted. Frankly, I'm impressed.

Scanner Comparison: Drum Scan

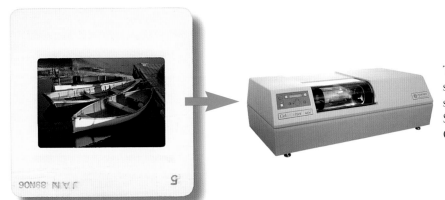

The 35mm slide was scanned at 2,000 spi using an Optronics Falcon drum scanner and saved as an RGB TIFF file. Scan courtesy of NancyScans, Inc., of Chatham, NY.

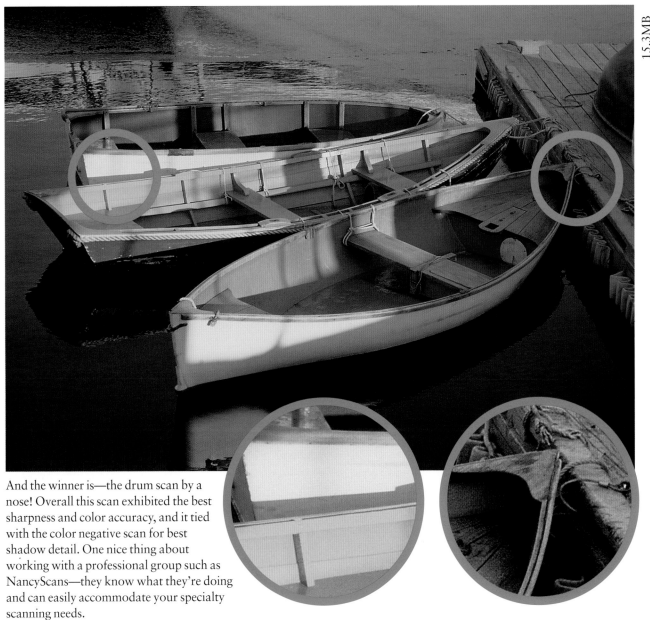

15.3MB

And the winner is—the drum scan by a nose! Overall this scan exhibited the best sharpness and color accuracy, and it tied with the color negative scan for best shadow detail. One nice thing about working with a professional group such as NancyScans—they know what they're doing and can easily accommodate your specialty scanning needs.

Types of Scans

Scanning for Screen

Increasingly, images are being scanned for multimedia purposes (i.e., computer display) as well as multiple media (computer display, digital prints, slides and print). For multiple media it's inappropriate to optimize an image for print, a procedure that can be done later. At the time of scanning, it's more important to capture as much data as possible at the highest possible gamut. For multiple media purposes, you need to scan an image to match the high resolution needed for print while also optimizing for the high color gamut of the computer screen.

A major problem with computer monitors is their lack of consistent color. The endless combination of cards and monitors also makes it impossible to predict the final image display size. This is particularly true on PCs since no standard yet exists for color management under Windows. Windows also has no way of knowing what kind of monitor is attached or what size it is.

The Macintosh is far more predictable because the cable that connects the monitor to the computer (generally) informs the system what size display is being used.

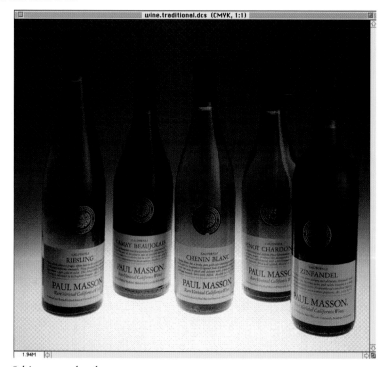

8-bit screen depth.

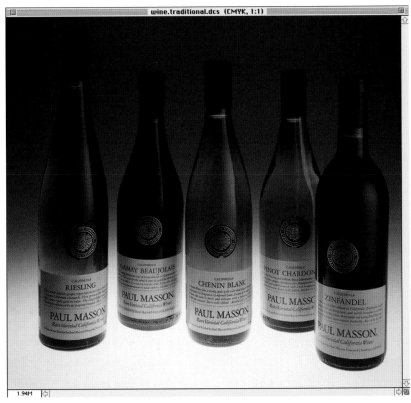

1.94M

16-bit screen depth.

Most Macintoshes display at around 72 ppi—although there are exceptions. ColorSync 2.1 is a professional-quality color management system available for all Macs.

Most monitors can display at least 256 colors (8 bit); in fact, 8-bit color can be found on almost all bargain-basement computers. However, 8-bit color needs to be dithered, making photos on these monitors somewhat "grainy." But if 8-bit images are adequate for your

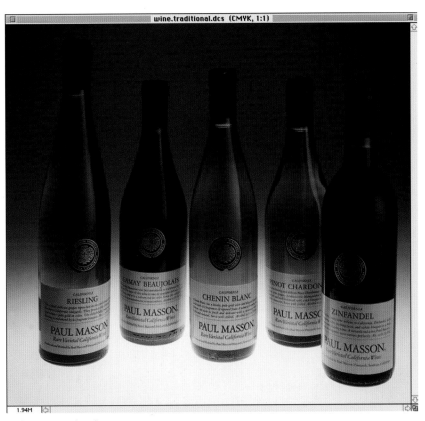

1.94M

24-bit screen depth.

needs (such as multimedia presentations), they are the most compatible across various systems—especially those that use the System Palette. Eight-bit images also take up very little disk space. For example, a 640 x 480 pixel, 8-bit image is only 300K in size, while a 640 x 480 pixel, 24-bit image is 900K—three times the size of the 8-bit image!

Fast becoming the multimedia standard are 16-bit depth computer monitors. Sixteen-bit displays are capable of 32,000 simultaneous colors (three 5-bit RGB channels plus one extra bit). Not only is 16 bit significantly better looking than 8 bit, it also displays a lot faster than 24 bit; in fact, in most cases, 16-bit images are indistinguishable on screen from equivalent 24-bit images. Someday all computer screens and high-definition televisions may be 24 bit. But in the meantime, 16 bit will become the universal cross-platform standard for the foreseeable future.

Of course, the granddaddy of all computer monitors is the big, 24-bit display. Although the size of 24-bit files (and the price of 24-bit display equipment) is enormous, nothing looks quite as good as a high-resolution 24-bit image—it is the closest you can come to the beauty and depth of a 35mm slide. However, it should be noted that this depth doesn't translate as effectively in print. Offset presses just can't print all

SCREEN SIZE	PIXEL DIMENSIONS OF SCREEN	APPROX. PIXELS PER INCH
8.5" (LCD)	640 x 480	94 ppi
9"	512 x 342	72 ppi
12"	512 x 384	63 ppi
	640 x 480	79 ppi
13"	640 x 480	72 ppi
	800 x 600	90 ppi
14"	640 x 480	66 ppi
	800 x 600	82 ppi
	832 x 624	86 ppi
15"	640 x 480	61 ppi
	800 x 600	76 ppi
	832 x 624	79 ppi
	1,024 x 768	98 ppi
16"	640 x 480	57 ppi
	800 x 600	71 ppi
	832 x 624	74 ppi
	1,024 x 768	91 ppi
17"	800 x 600	66 ppi
	832 x 624	69 ppi
	1,024 x 768	85 ppi
19"	800 x 600	58 ppi
	832 x 624	61 ppi
	1,024 x 768	75 ppi
20"	1,024 x 768	71 ppi
	1,152 x 870	79 ppi
21"	1,024 x 768	67 ppi
	1,152 x 870	75 ppi

Use this table for calculating final sizes of scanned images for screen display.

the colors you see on screen. If you find yourself wanting to print a 24-bit image, consult Photoshop's Gamut Alarm in the Color Palette to see which colors won't reproduce effectively on press.

For information on FPO and halftone scanning see page 11.

Scanning for OCR

Most OCR software is optimized for 300 spi and 1-bit black and white. 300 spi is more than enough resolution to distinguish normal text on a page. OCR software relies on pattern matching instead of raw resolution. Thus, using grayscale or a higher sampling rate only slows things down without providing much (if any) increase in accuracy.

Scanning for Autotracing

For autotracing purposes only one thing counts—the highest possible resolution. Autotracing algorithms attempt to match the best possible curve to a jagged bitmap outline. Thus, the more bits, the better the matching. If you are stuck with a low-resolution scan or scanner (300 spi or less), you may want to try the increased resolution technique shown on page 102, before attempting to autotrace it.

WHEN AUTOTRACING, SCAN AT A HIGH RESOLUTION

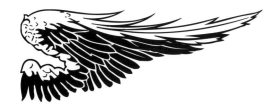

Autotraced copy of an image scanned at 600 spi.

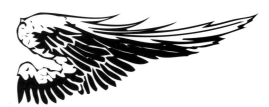

Autotraced copy of the same image scanned at 200 spi.

Types of Scanning-Related Software

Plug-Ins

Plug-in software refers to any application (often called an "applet") that can be launched from within another "host" program. Examples of host programs are Photoshop, QuarkXPress and Streamline. Examples of plug-ins are the vast majority of scanning applications.

Most scanning software today is either TWAIN or Photoshop Acquire compatible. Add-in utilities that utilize such standards can deliver the scans right where you need them most—in your favorite image-editing program.

Scanning plug-ins control your scanner and allow you to crop, size, and correct for color, tone, contrast and lightness. The following plug-in options help you clean up, color correct and apply special effects to an image "post-scan" within a dedicated image-editing program:

- Special effect filters such as Kai's Power Tools and Adobe Gallery Effects can add all sorts of photographic, fractal and painterly effects to your images after you scan.

- Noise-reduction plug-ins shipping with Agfa scanners and others allow you to reduce noise in your scans (as well as in scans supplied to you). It's generally better to use these plug-ins sparingly, for example, in the shadow areas only.

- Import/export/acquire filters allow you to export or import an image with a unique file format.

- Image enhancers such as MonacoColor and Intellihance analyze an image by looking for statistical relationships within the data and modifying the image to provide optimal density, exposure, saturation and sharpness.

- Scanner calibration packages such as Linocolor and ColorAccess provide color calibration on the fly from within Photoshop—important for quality work since your scanner changes slightly from month to month and even from day to day. Calibration software scans a known target and creates new lookup tables.

- Agfa's FotoTune CMYK Photoshop ColorLinker provides better RGB-to-CMYK conversions than Photoshop's internal algorithms.

System Level Software

There are a number of system-level programs out there offering color correction capabilities. These programs, called color management systems (CMS), enable your system to calibrate itself so that the colorspace defined by the scanner is correctly mapped to the colorspace available on the monitor, which, in turn, is correctly mapped to the output device. In effect, using a CMS allows all the devices to process color in a definable, predictable manner. Here are descriptions of some of the more popular CMS options available at the time of this writing.

- Apple's ColorSync has quietly become the standard color management platform upon which to build more comprehensive solutions. ColorSync provides the basic building blocks needed for all applications and hardware to "talk" to one another using the same colorspace language. Because Windows 3.x doesn't offer equivalent system-level color management, the Macintosh has established an enormous lead in regards to high-end color management solutions. ColorSync will eventually be available to Windows users.

- Pantone and Light Source have teamed up to provide one of the most comprehensive color management systems around. Pantone Open Color Environment (POCE) is designed to match both continuous-tone images as well as spot colors (i.e., the ubiquitous Pantone Matching System, or PMS). All current licensees of Pantone colors (Quark, Adobe, Altsys, Corel, etc.) ship POCE with their products.

- Packaged on a single CD-ROM, Linocolor Profilers give you all the tools you need to generate ICC profiles for your image capture, display and output devices.

- Kodak signed deals with Adobe and others to license its version of a CMS, which they call KCMS. Although promising, KCMS has yet to prove its mettle since it is currently incompatible with other CMS solutions. If you own one of Adobe's products, such as Photoshop or PageMaker, you probably have a KCMS folder sitting somewhere on your computer taking up space and waiting to be utilized.

- Agfa's FotoFlow color management system allows you to characterize your scanner by comparing a scan of an IT8 test target to supplied reference data, and then it builds a conversion linker to the RGB or CMYK output of your choice. Like KCMS, it is currently incompatible with other CMS solutions, but Agfa and most of the other CMS developers have promised to be ColorSync 2 compatible, thus paving the way for future compatibility.

Stand-Alone

Dedicated stand-alone software is set up this way because it is simply too complex to launch from a host program. Most stand-alone applications are unique products offering highly specialized features. Be aware that running these programs concurrently with other programs requires a computer setup with lots of RAM, large hard disks and a multitasking operating system like Windows NT, UNIX or System 8.0 for Macintosh.

- Fractal Design Painter offers unique painterly image-editing tools not available anywhere else—everything from van Gogh effects to watercolor to "blobs" that distort an image in unique and unusual ways.

- Live Picture from Live Picture, Inc., is unique in that it uses a special mathematical file format called FITS that allows users to open 200MB images in about ten seconds! What's more, Live Picture offers unlimited layers and infinite resolution. Final, placeable, printable images are RIPped (to TIFF or EPS) from within Live Picture to match the exact resolution of the intended output device. Live Picture requires at least 64MB RAM, a host machine and lots of hard disk space!

- ColorSynergy, from Canada, brings fast, accurate color to all components of a Macintosh-based desktop system. ColorSynergy provides a set of color management tools for color calibrating a Macintosh and all of its associated imaging devices including scanners, monitors and printers, with or without color measuring instruments. Compatible with Color Tron II and X-rite colorimeters. Candela is also making its rich color source code C program library available to OEMs for Macintosh, Windows, Sun Sparc and SGI platforms.

- PixelCraft ColorAccess is a full-featured color correcting, separation utility. It's popular with professional color separators because it uses terminology and controls they are familiar with. By and large it supports midlevel and high-end scanners, but your scanner may support it as well. It also comes bundled with high-end scanners such as the Sharp JX-610 and the PixelCraftPro Imager 8000.

OCR

Optical character recognition (OCR) software is the workhorse of office scanner tools. As its name implies, OCR software uses the bitmap image generated by a scanner to capture an "image" of a page of text and, using complex pattern-matching algorithms, interprets the series of scanner samples into individual letterforms. The result is a page of (mostly) accurate text.

OCR works best with unkerned, amply leaded body text. Dot-matrix and fax input text can confuse even the best OCR software. Although some high-end OCR applications boast of 99 percent accuracy, be forewarned: This means that a typical page of text (2,000 to 3,000 characters) may have twenty to thirty errors—errors you have to fix manually or catch later with a spelling checker.

Look for learning capability so that your OCR setup can obtain better results over time using your specific combination of scanner and input text style. Also look for automatic document feeder support if your scanner has that option.

Utilities

There are beaucoup utilities out there for scanner operators. Most offer complementary functions to those that are standard for image-editing and scanning programs.

- Adobe Streamline is the de facto raster-to-vector (also known as autotrace) conversion utility for desktop systems. Not only does it work with black-and-white and grayscale images, it also converts color image files into line art, with unique and pleasing results. Because it supports Photoshop plug-ins, you can scan directly from within Streamline.
- Sizing calculators, available online or as downloadable shareware from major bulletin boards, can assist you in determining the optimal size parameters to use for scanning without guesswork. A good example is the scanning calculator available at http://www.hsdesign.com/scancalc.
- DeBabelizer from Equilibrium Technologies imports, converts and exports more than forty-five image file formats from the Mac, PC, Amiga, Apple II, Photo CD and Silicon Graphics computers.

File Formats & Storage

Types of File Formats

When saving images, the file types used most are TIFF and EPS. All image-editing applications, and most scanning software, support these two formats (TIFF and EPS):

TIFF (tagged image file format) is probably the most widely used bitmapped file format. It can be imported into a wide variety of page layout, image-editing, illustration and even word processing programs. It works for all types of images, line art and halftones as well as color or grayscale, and it can have a bit depth of 1, 4, 24 or 32 bits. There are Mac and PC versions as well. Version 4.0 of the TIFF specification is the most compatible, while version 5.0 offers added compression and higher bit depths. The 6.0 version specification allows for high-fidelity color and even greater compression. Although TIFF images are extremely versatile, older programs sometimes aren't able to import files using newer versions of the TIFF specification.

EPS (encapsulated PostScript) is as popular as TIFF for saving image files and it works for as many types of images as TIFF. EPS files can be imported into nearly every kind of application, from page layout to word processing. EPS is commonly specified when converting an RGB file to CMYK to create five-color separation files—one for each of the four process colors and one for position only. This five-file EPS format is also known as DCS (digital color separation). EPS is also very useful for saving RGB files that need to be output to slide recorders. Its main drawback is that EPS takes up more disk space than any other format.

The following are other option formats:

BMP (short for bitmap) is a basic, no-frills, Windows-only format that's generally used for screen display. Most Windows C programs can use BMP files when compiling applications to run on Windows computers. For this reason, most Windows applications support this format.

PICT (short for picture) is a proprietary Mac format generally used for screen display only. Some Mac programs, such as Adobe Illustrator and Macromedia Director, can only import images saved as either PICT or EPS. Because it doesn't provide information for separations, PICT shouldn't be used for printed images.

JPEG (Joint Photographic Experts Group) is a compression format that makes very compact files and is a great way to exchange data with your clients and vendors because its small file size allows speedy transmission via modem. However, this option uses lossy technology to compress files, so you may want to save a master version of the file before saving it as a JPEG image. (See Compression, on the following page, for an explanation of lossy technology.)

GIF is an 8-bit (256-color) palette-based file format used primarily for the World Wide Web.

PNG, known as "ping," is a variable-bit, multipurpose, high-compression file format designed especially for the World Wide Web.

PCX is an early low-end PC standard that is still being used today by some image-editing programs, such as Windows Paint and PC Paintbrush. Because of its early adoption, many other Windows applications support this format.

TARGA is an early high-end PC standard developed by AT&T. Although quite popular with video editing and multimedia, it hasn't gained wide acceptance in the prepress field mostly because of the overwhelming popularity of TIFF and EPS.

PHOTOSHOP NATIVE Quite a few image-editing programs now support the Photoshop native file format, including Fractal Design Painter. Adobe PageMaker also supports this format. Photoshop native files take up less space than uncompressed TIFF files and are faster to open and save than compressed TIFF files. Photoshop native also allows you to save masks, clipping paths and alpha channels.

Compression

You need to compress large images whenever you run out of room on your hard disk. If you use your scanner as much as I do, you may run out of hard disk space on a daily basis! You may also find it convenient to compress images to send files to your clients and vendors, particularly via modem. Two types of compression are available: *lossless* and *lossy*.

LOSSLESS compression does just what it implies—nothing is lost during compression. Using mathematical algorithms that eliminate redundant data, lossless compression often provides significant compression with reasonable performance. Examples of lossless compression are Photoshop native format, TIFF 6.0 and compression utilities such as StuffIt and PKZIP. Some files have very little redundant data, so compressing them with a lossless scheme can actually increase the file size! Lossless compression is often used when archiving a file for backup. In fact, backup software such as Retrospect offers both software and hardware compression (if available on that particular device) when archiving.

LOSSY compression offers even greater image compression. The trade-off is that it results in loss of data during the compression process. The theory is that certain data is not important in an image and consequently is expendable. In practice, you can usually tell if a file has been compressed with a lossy scheme by examining flat color areas near the border of transitional colors. Depending on the original and also on how much compression you specify (high, medium or low), the effect can be subtle or irritating.

However, results are often gratifying. I recently compressed an image using JPEG from 3MB to 300K! By using JPEG compression in the Quality = Good mode, I was able to reduce the file size significantly while retaining nearly the same quality the image had without compression. You'd be hard-pressed to tell the difference (see figures on page 69). I was able to quickly send this low-memory file via modem to my service bureau for color prints, as well as to my client for approval. The file transfer took one-tenth the time it would have if I hadn't compressed it.

Lossy compression is very popular with multimedia professionals—most notably when delivered by Apple QuickTime—and like it or not, it's here to stay.

Lossy Compression

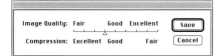

This setting was used to reduce the file size using JPEG compression.

Compressed to 90K, this image is of fair quality.

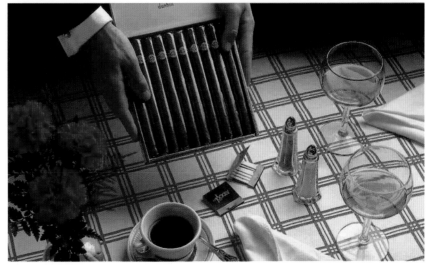

Compressed to 270K the same image is far more acceptable.

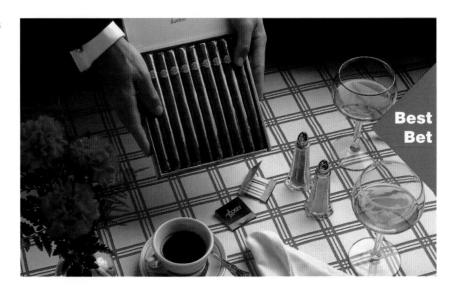

At 1,040K, this compression yielded excellent results; however, for obtaining client approval over the modem, the smaller 270K file is perfectly acceptable.

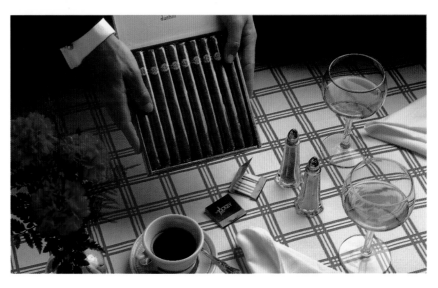

Calibrating Your System (Properly)

The proper way to calibrate your system is to purchase additional specialty hardware and software to help get your system in perfect harmony. The basic items:

- A system-level ICC-compatible color management system, such as Apple's professional-quality ColorSync 2.1

- A special piece of hardware called a densitometer for accurately calibrating your monitor and any resultant targets created by the software (see below). A popular example is the Light Source Colortron II (shown at right).

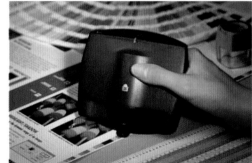

- Calibration software for creating ICC targets that get output on a variety of print devices and then are read by the densitometer to create a profile for that target. An excellent example is ColorSynergy 2.0 from Candela.

Step 1

Install ICC-compatible color management system software.

Step 2

Install software and hardware for densitometer. Calibrate your monitor with densitometer following the manufacturer's instructions. Create a profile for your monitor, save it and install it as the default profile for your monitor to be used by the color management system.

Step 3

Install calibration software. Scan an IT8 target on the desired scanner. IT8 targets are available for both reflective and transparency scanners. Have calibration software analyze the resultant scan to create the profile for the scanner(s).

Step 4

Print IT8 target image on desired printer. Measure the test pattern with the densitometer. Note: Some densitometers can do this in a single pass! The Colortron II mentioned previously requires that you capture each color cell on the target—a laborious undertaking. When you're done, save the profile for the printer.

All done!

Your system is now calibrated as a "closed loop." As you add new devices, you'll need to calibrate each new device. You'll also have to occasionally recalibrate your older devices as they age.

Also, remember to save your TIFF images with an ICC header whenever possible (you may need special software to do that). In that way, service providers and others can use your images in the way you intended, even though you didn't explicitly create calibrations for their devices.

Calibrating Your Monitor (On the Cheap)

Figure 1: The Gamma control panel.

If you don't own one of the proprietary color management systems described in this chapter, be prepared to roll up your sleeves and do a lot of grunt work. Here's how to do a basic system calibration with Photoshop:

Step 1

Launch Gamma (supplied with Photoshop) from the control panel. Set the Gamma to 1.8. Adjust the slider until the gray bar is of a smooth, continuous tone. Adjust the White Point and Balance to compensate for any color cast your monitor may have. Save the settings. Quit.

Step 2

Launch Photoshop. Load the CMYK file Olé No Moiré (supplied with Photoshop). Under File/Preferences, choose the Monitor Setup dialog box. Choose your monitor and manufacturer from the list, or choose default if yours isn't listed. Click OK. Make sure the Colors dialog box is open and RGB is selected. Use the Eye Dropper tool to select the upper right-hand 50 percent gray area of Olé No Moiré.

Figure 2: The Monitor Setup dialog box under File/Preferences.

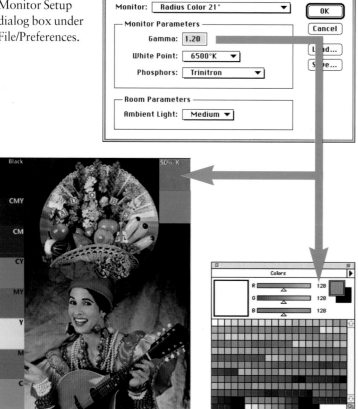

Figure 3: The Olé No Moiré image.

Figure 4: The Colors palette.

Step 3

The RGB colors should be exactly 128, 128, 128. If not, go back to the Monitor Setup dialog box and adjust the Gamma setting up or down so the gray reading of the CMYK file in RGB colors is as shown in the Olé No Moiré image. Go back one more time to the Monitor Setup dialog box and save your settings as MyMonitor.Settings.

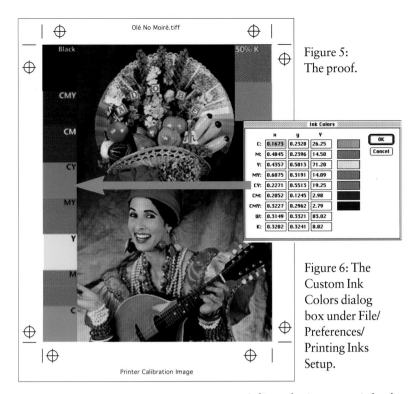

Figure 5: The proof.

Figure 6: The Custom Ink Colors dialog box under File/ Preferences/ Printing Inks Setup.

Step 4

Choose Printing Inks Setup under File/ Preferences. Set the printing inks to SWOP if you intend to print to an offset press.

Step 5

Choose Separation Setup under File/ Preferences. Select GCR unless you are printing on newsprint.

Step 6

Load into Photoshop an RGB scan you want to separate. Adjust the image so it looks good on your now-calibrated monitor. Change Mode to CMYK, to create separations using your specific calibration settings. Use the LEVELS command to adjust for press conditions, such as dot gain. Save the file as a TIFF or five-file EPS file. Also save Olé No Moiré as a TIFF or five-file EPS file. Place both images in your page layout program. Send the files to your service bureau and order an Iris Ink Jet or film separations with Matchprint proof (or equivalent).

Step 7

Compare the proof(s) with the image displayed on your monitor. If you have properly calibrated your monitor, the proof should be a good match to what you see on screen. If not, you may need to do one more step.

Step 8

Choose Printing Inks under File/Preferences. Select Custom Inks instead of SWOP and the Ink Colors dialog box will appear. Using a densitometer, enter the x, y and Y values (CIE color coordinates) taken from the proof for each of the seven colors shown.

If you don't have access to a densitometer, adjust the colors by eye. Click on each color patch and then adjust the color on screen until it matches your proof. Click OK and repeat for each color patch. Save your Printing Ink settings and reseparate your RGB file by converting the mode to CMYK. When you compare again, you should have an exact match.

Calibrating Your Printer (On the Cheap)

Sometimes even calibrating your monitor (as described previously) doesn't work with a particular printer. The images always come out too dark no matter what you do. Don't fret. Rather than purchase expensive calibration software and hardware, here's a simple, foolproof way to do a basic printer calibration with Photoshop.

Assuming you have calibrated your monitor, as described earlier, adjust the image to the way you want it to look when it prints. (Remember, of course, that not all colors you see on screen can be printed.) Reduce the image's dimensions to half its print size (e.g., 4" x 5" for an 8" x 10" proof). Next, double the Canvas Size (i.e., 200 percent width and height) and place the image in the top left corner. Make a duplicate of the image and place a copy of it in each of the three remaining corners of the canvas. Now, since most printers print darker than what you see on screen, select each of the alternate images and adjust each to a slightly different setting using Photoshop's LEVELS command.

In this example I have chosen to demonstrate the effect of adjusting the Midtone brightness (also called Gamma) setting at 1.2, 1.4 and 1.6. Although the effect on screen looks washed out, I'm not concerned with that. I'm only concerned with how it looks *when printed*. You may need to set the Output Highlight dot and Output Shadow dot settings as well, depending on your printer's recommendation (see page 21). This creates a basis for comparing what settings give you the best output for your particular printer. In this example (using a Fujix Picrography RGB device) Gamma 1.6 gave consistently good results from my monitor for any image I could see on my screen.

Lastly, convert to CMYK (if necessary) and save as a TIFF or EPS file for print output. Note: You'll have to perform the above test for each printer you intend to print to, but this simple procedure will save you from pulling out your hair in the future!

What you see on screen.

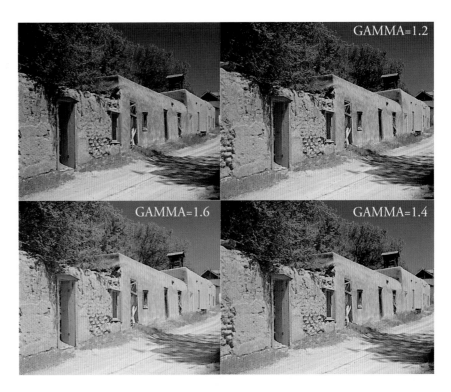

What you see on your proof.

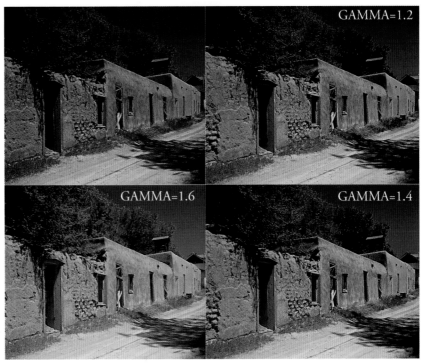

CHAPTER THREE

The Scanner Workout

Ways to Eliminate Moirés

A moiré is a wavelike pattern that occurs whenever two or more regular patterns are superimposed on one another. Moirés occur when you attempt to scan something that has already been halftoned—an image that has already been printed in a magazine, newspaper, book, etc. (see Legal and Ethical Issues in chapter five for more information on what can and cannot be legally scanned and copied).

One way to eliminate a moiré is to use hardware and/or software that automatically descreens an image during the scanning process. One program for doing this is FotoLook, a scanning program with automatic sharpening and descreening that comes with the Agfa Arcus Plus scanner. It works particularly well with color halftone images. If you work with a lot of preprinted images, the "push-button" convenience of these packages may be well worth the investment.

Those of you who don't have an Agfa scanner can eliminate the moiré in an image-editing program such as Photoshop using a variety of filters and sharpening. Halftone images all respond differently to scanning, and sometimes only certain combinations of filters produce optimum results. Rest assured, the results are equal to and possibly better than the automatic solutions.

Don't expect to get more resolution or detail out of a halftone image than the lpi of the original. The best you can expect from your scan is to equal, but never improve upon, the original halftone.

A different kind of moiré occurs when you print black-and-white computer screen shots, particularly where a patterned background occurs. You can correct this by scanning the image at an spi number that is a factor of the final printed resolution. For example, if you're printing an image at a resolution of 1,200 dpi you should scan it at 75, 100, 120, 150, 200, 300, 400 or 600 spi. The trick is that these numbers all divide evenly into 1,200, and, thus, no moiré is introduced by the halftoning process. Manipulate the image in an image-editing program as described in this demo for eliminating moirés in traditional halftones.

Ways to Eliminate Moirés

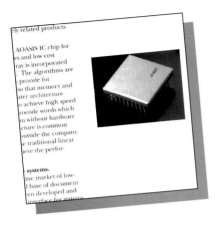

ORIGINAL

This black-and-white photo of a computer chip was clipped from a high-tech brochure. It needs to be scanned, rescreened and reprinted at its original size.

Prescreened images should be scanned at an spi that is twice the halftone frequency or lpi of the halftone image. The optimum scan for an image clipped from a magazine is 266 spi, twice the typical 133 lpi of magazine halftone screens. A newspaper image should be scanned at 130 spi, or twice the typical 65 lpi of a newspaper halftone. Don't scan at a resolution higher than what's necessary to do the job, because the descreening process is optimized for a 2-to-1 sample rate. Besides, scanning an image at a resolution of more than 300 spi creates an unnecessarily large file and requires additional RAM to handle.

Because this image is a 150-lpi halftone, it should be scanned at 300 spi (a 2:1 ratio) and scaled at twice the size (200 percent) of the original to maximize detail and provide the best sampling rate for the descreening procedures depicted.

Using Photoshop's Gaussian Blur and Sharpening

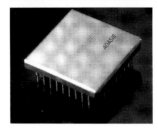

STEP 1

When the photo is first scanned, a significant moiré appears in the dot pattern.

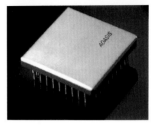

STEP 2

Apply the Gaussian Blur filter and Sharpening tool. Gaussian Blur works best when it is assigned a radius of 1.0 to 2.0 pixels.

Using Agfa Arcus Plus and FotoLook

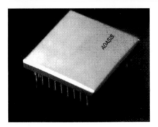

STEP 1

This 300-spi image is the result of selecting automatic sharpening and descreening before scanning.

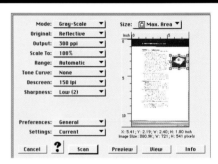

Descreening was set at 150 lpi and Sharpness was set at low.

Using Photoshop's Despeckle Filter

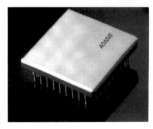

STEP 1

The Despeckle filter is applied to the same 2:1 scan used above. This results in a slight improvement. You can also try applying the Median filter, especially useful with color images. Halftone images respond differently to scanning. Sometimes only certain combinations of filters produce optimal results.

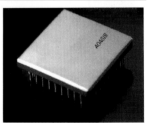

STEP 2

Apply a 50 percent scale reduction to the despeckled image and the results aren't bad. Although the final image seems as though it could benefit from some sharpening, don't try it. Because the Despeckle filter didn't actually get rid of the moiré, the Sharpening tool would only accentuate the noise.

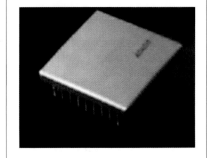

Starting with a 1:1 scan (where a 150-lpi halftone was scanned in at 150 spi) yields less than satisfactory results.

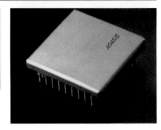

STEP 2, continued

A setting too high, such as 3.0, destroys the detail in the image. Use 1.5 for most scanning applications.

STEP 3

Reduce by 50 percent and apply the Sharpening tool again. The final image, output at the same size as the original clipping, has a resolution of 150 dpi.

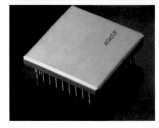

STEP 2

A 50 percent reduction to 150 spi plus sharpening in Photoshop yielded this halftone.

Tip

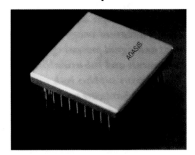

It's important to remember that thin, nonopaque paper allows whatever ink there is on the back to show through. To prevent this, use black paper behind your image when scanning. You may need to compensate for muddy or darkened whites created by the black paper showing through by adjusting the gamma or contrast levels of the image in your scanning software or later in an image-editing program such as Photoshop.

Finding Your Scanner's "Sweet Spot"

Most scanners have minor inconsistencies. Given this tendency, it should come as no surprise to realize there are some portions of the imaging area of your scanner that are better than others. If possible, you should space your image within this "sweet spot" to obtain the best and most consistent scans.

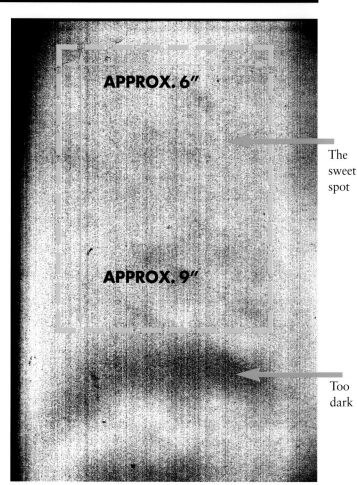

STEP 1
To find your own sweet spot, simply make a scan of the entire image area (my scanner's live image area is 8½" x 14", 21.6cm x 35.6cm) using a clean, white surface, such as a sheet of opaque paper, to scan. Set the resolution low, between 72 and 100 spi. (For this demo, there's no need to make a high-memory scan.)

STEP 2
Bring the image into an image-editing program such as Photoshop and use the Equalize command to exaggerate any minor differences within the image area. As you can see, my scanner has dark spots on the edges as well as a bright streak on the left. The blotchy area about eleven inches down also is something I need to be aware of when scanning subtle images.

Once you've determined where your scanner's sweet spot is, you may want to make a cardboard template to aid you in future scanning.

Correcting Poor Color

Shooting a picture in poor lighting conditions often results in an image that has an unnatural color cast. But fear not, it's easier to color-correct an image in the computer than it is in the darkroom. The surefire way to get outstanding scans every time is to scan first with no tone controls (gamma = 1). Then use the Curves command in an image-editing program to adjust the curves of the image to where the color should be. Save the curve and rescan using Import Curves. You'll get a great image when you scan this time.

STEP 1
I increased contrast in the shadows dramatically by bringing the image into Photoshop and adjusting its curve as shown.

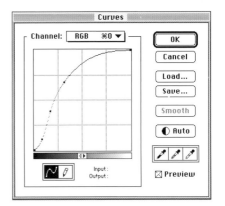

STEP 2
I also added warmth to the picture by separately adjusting the red curve to give it more dominance.

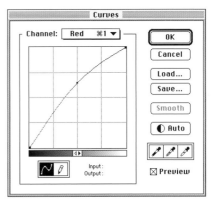

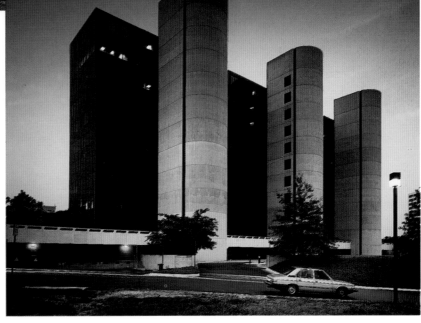

ORIGINAL
This particular image is not only too dark, it's also too blue because it was shot at dusk. The length of the exposure also resulted in reciprocity failure—a consequence of using film not designed to work in low light conditions.

STEP 3
After saving the curve adjustments, I rescanned using the imported curve. A second scan produced this much improved image.

Scanning at Higher Than Optical Resolution

When you choose a resolution that goes beyond the stated optical resolution of your scanner, it's important to consider the orientation of your image before scanning.

Most flatbed scanners offer asymmetric optical scanning. (Many slide scanners are assymetrical as well.) For such flatbeds, typical "true" optical resolutions are 300 spi horizontal and 600 spi vertical. Higher-priced flatbeds may offer "true" optical resolutions of 600 spi horizontal and 1,200 spi vertical. Because your image-editing program needs square samples to work with, flatbed engineers resort to a sleight of hand: They interpolate the horizontal data up to match the vertical resolution, in effect "doubling" the horizontal data. As a result, when you scan beyond your scanner's maximum optical resolution, you're not getting "real" data but "best guess" or "faked" data for the horizontal data.

There is a way you can minimize this effect. When scanning at a higher than true optical resolution, be sure the longest dimension of your rectangular image matches the higher optical number. If you have a 4" x 6" (10.2cm x 11.4cm) photo, orient it on the scanner by aligning the longest dimension of the photo parallel to the dimension that has the higher optical resolution. For most scanners this is the vertical (sometimes referred to as "slower") dimension. Note: Square images generally are not affected by orientation because there is no net gain to be made by rotating them.

The net result for a rectangular image with a length-to-width ratio of 2:1 is up to 25 percent more "real" data—even though the file sizes are the same!

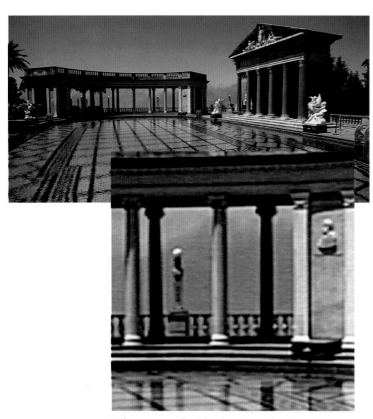

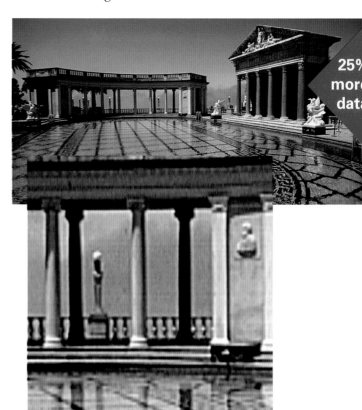

When scanned with a horizontal orientation at 1,200 spi, most of this image's data is captured on its longest dimension at the scanner's maximum optical resolution of 600 spi. The resulting 1,200-spi visual is made from a 50/50 split of "real" and "faked" data.

When rotated 90°, with its longest dimension on the vertical axis, and scanned at 1,200 spi, the same image is made up of more "real" data because most of it was captured at the scanner's "stepped" resolution of 1,200 spi. The detail in this image is significantly better, though the file sizes are the same.

Choosing Optimal Color Bit Depth for GIF Files

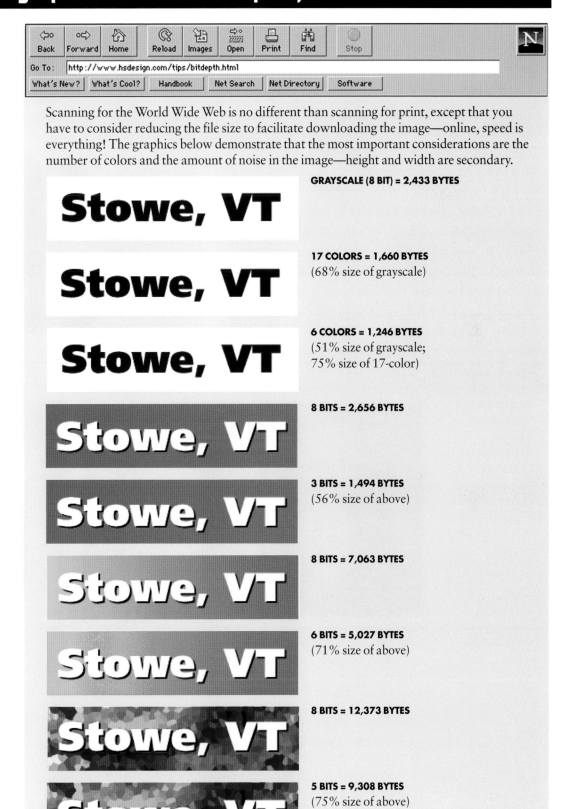

Scanning for the World Wide Web is no different than scanning for print, except that you have to consider reducing the file size to facilitate downloading the image—online, speed is everything! The graphics below demonstrate that the most important considerations are the number of colors and the amount of noise in the image—height and width are secondary.

GRAYSCALE (8 BIT) = 2,433 BYTES

17 COLORS = 1,660 BYTES
(68% size of grayscale)

6 COLORS = 1,246 BYTES
(51% size of grayscale;
75% size of 17-color)

8 BITS = 2,656 BYTES

3 BITS = 1,494 BYTES
(56% size of above)

8 BITS = 7,063 BYTES

6 BITS = 5,027 BYTES
(71% size of above)

8 BITS = 12,373 BYTES

5 BITS = 9,308 BYTES
(75% size of above)

Scanning 3-D Objects

You can use your flatbed scanner to capture 3-D objects much as a camera would. (Assuming, of course, they fit on the glass platen!)

Shown here are just a few of the many things I have scanned over the years. What is particularly nice is how fast and easy it is to obtain "photos" this way. Plus, the images are yours—no rights need to be negotiated for any of your scanned "photos."

The obvious problem with scanning 3-D objects is lack of lighting control. Most flatbed scanners capture some of the dimensionality of an object by casting a slight shadow. (See the diagram of how a scanner works on page 8 in chapter one.) The direction of the shadow depends on the optics of your particular scanner and where the object is placed on the glass platen. You have to experiment with your scanner to see where shadows fall each time an object is repositioned.

SCANNING FOOD
The most important thing to remember is to clean up afterward. Other than that, you'll be impressed at how good food looks when scanned. The soft, natural shadows created by the scanner are very close to the effect of studio lighting.

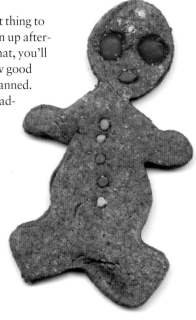

SCANNING CYLINDRICAL OBJECTS
Before you begin to scan, prevent the object from rolling around by taping the back of it to a large piece of paper—in this case, I used white bristol board. The paper serves as the background of the object while it's being scanned.

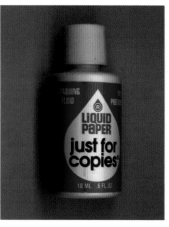

STEP 1
Determine where you want the shadow to fall on your image by making a preliminary scan. Reposition the object and its backing on the scanning bed if the shadowed side of your image isn't exactly where you want it to be. To create a lighter shadow, apply additional lighting by positioning a light source (such as a table lamp) underneath the lid, close to the object, resting on the platen. Be careful when doing this—table lamps can get very hot!

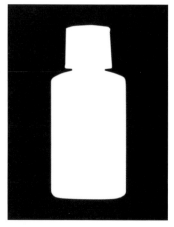

STEP 2
Use channel masks in an image-editing program such as Photoshop, to change the background. First, mask the object by using the selection marquee and the option key to create a continuous selection path. When the object is selected, save the selection to a channel, invert it (to select the background region), and use the gradient fill tool to fill the background with a smooth blend.

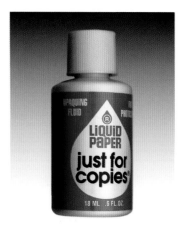

STEP 3
The final result is equivalent to the effect of studio lighting at a fraction of the cost.

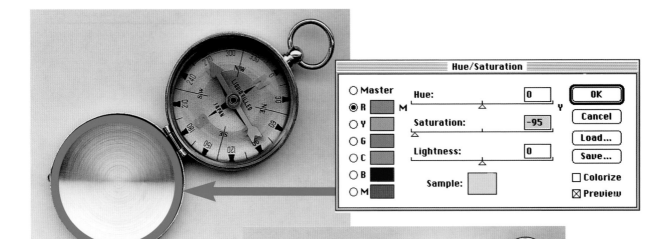

Hue/Saturation		
○ Master	Hue: `0`	OK
⦿ R ▢ M		Cancel
○ Y ▢	Saturation: `-95`	Load...
○ G ▢		Save...
○ C ▢	Lightness: `0`	
○ B ▢		☐ Colorize
○ M ▢	Sample: ▢	☒ Preview

SCANNING METALLIC OBJECTS

Color scans of metallic objects inevitably produce rainbow patterns in some portions of your image, similar to what's shown above.

To remove the rainbow, bring your image into Photoshop and select the rainbowed regions. Open the Hue/Saturation controls and individually select the red, green and blue, reducing the saturation of each as shown.

Keep in mind that if you scan at 1,200 spi or more, you can enlarge any object for high-resolution output. This 1,200-spi scan of a dime, output at 600 percent and 133 lpi, yielded this highly detailed image. When you need a close-up of a tiny object, the scanner works much better than a camera with a macro lens—much faster, too.

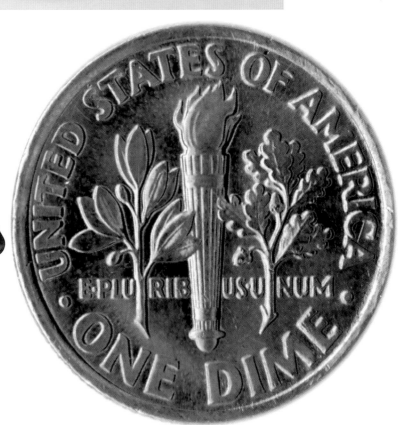

Scanning Great Background Effects

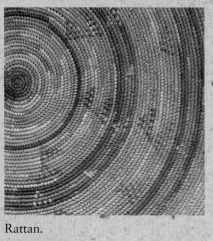

Rattan.

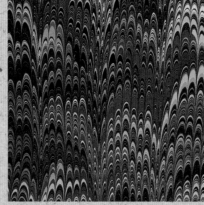

Marbled paper.

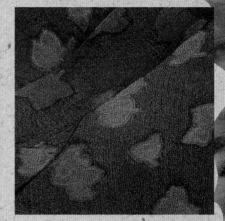

Silk scarf.

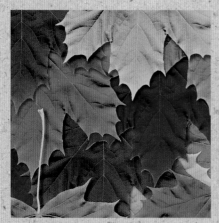

Leaves.

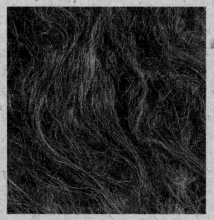

Wool blanket.

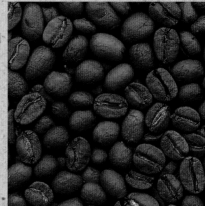

Coffee beans.

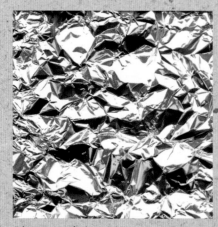

Aluminum foil.

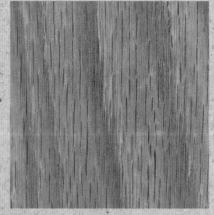

Wood.

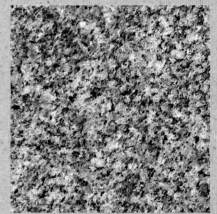

Granite.

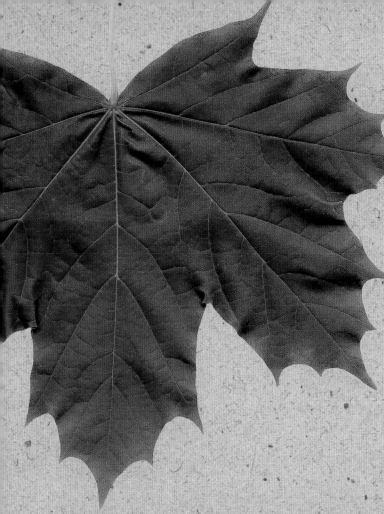

One of the most versatile uses of your scanner is in producing interesting background effects by scanning objects and textures. You can create your own library of ready-to-use, copyright-free images that can add depth and visual interest to projects that have no photo budget. Often the quality of these images is superior to what you would achieve using a studio camera and lights.

An endless variety of backgrounds is possible—everything from leaves to coffee beans to wood siding can make an appealing backdrop for a catchy headline or block of text. You can also create unique abstract effects by bringing scanned images into an image-editing program where you can posterize them or add a filter.

Fabric and paper textures yield great results. My favorite trick is to scan recycled papers for use in four-color print projects where I want a softer, more textural look on a coated paper.

The key to successful scans is keeping your scanner clean. You don't want kiwifruit juice getting into your scanner's electronic mechanisms! After scanning the great outdoors, take the time to clean your equipment.

In general, backgrounds are best scanned at 100 percent. You should also save them at the same frequency as the intended output. I typically scan at 300 spi, but this level of resolution usually results in a file of at least 20MB for an 8½" x 11" (12.6cm x 27.9cm) scan! For less detailed imagery, you may be able to make do with a lower resolution, but for highly detailed material, nothing less will do.

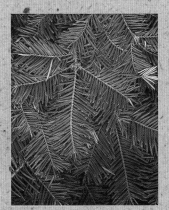
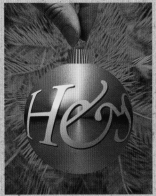

Black-and-white scan.   Final composite.

Even black-and-white scanners can be used to generate color backgrounds. To make our holiday greeting card, I scanned some pine swags on my black-and-white scanner and then converted the scan to an RGB image in Photoshop. After I changed the overall color to green, I added other holiday images.

Tip

If you're planning to overprint text on a four-color background scan, the scan should be light enough to maintain text legibility. For this reason, it's wise to eliminate the black screen when you convert the scan to CMYK. This increases the contrast of black text overprinting the background and facilitates copy revisions on the black (text) film without affecting the background image.

In Photoshop you can easily create a custom color separation that eliminates the black screen by selecting Preferences/Separation Setup (under the File menu). Choose GCR and set the black replacement to None. Then convert your RGB file to CMY(empty K) and voilà, a color separation with no black dot!

Scanning High-Key Images

High-key images are those that have most of the data in the highlight to midtone regions. It's important to note that high-key images are meant to be light, as opposed to an image that is overexposed or faded (see Salvaging a Faded Original on page 104 for more information on restoring a faded photograph). You don't want to "rescue" a high-key image—you just want to make sure it will reproduce at its best.

To achieve optimum results when scanning a high-key original such as this, the objective is to end up with clean whites while still retaining detail in other portions of the image. You may find an initial scan yields a satisfactory high-key image, and you may not need to go through the steps outlined in this demo. However, if you need to make adjustments, and your scanning software supports it, you can create a new tone curve and use it to achieve a better image when scanning.

I scanned the image in this demo with no tone corrections and then brought it into Photoshop to determine the optimal tone curve. After saving the revised tone curve and importing it into my scanning software, I was able to rescan this image for optimal data capture.

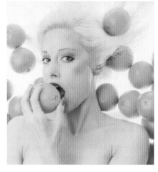

ORIGINAL

This 35mm slide of an ultra-fair model with lemons is almost as high-key as the classic "polar bear in a blizzard." A histogram of the image verifies this, showing a concentration of data in the highlight regions on the far right portion of the scale.

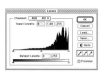

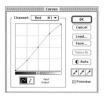

STEP 1

After bringing the image into Photoshop, you may need to adjust the overall tone of the image. To do this, choose the Curves command and adjust the RGB channel curve to emphasize the highlights (gamma = 0.75). The curve shown for this particular image increases the contrast in the highlight region, making the midtones slightly darker—just what you want.

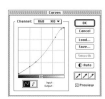

STEP 2

In this case, I also selected the red channel of the curve and adjusted it slightly to make the flesh tones warmer. Save the curve to disk and label it High Key Curve or a similar identifier.

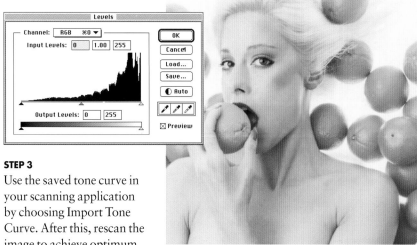

STEP 3

Use the saved tone curve in your scanning application by choosing Import Tone Curve. After this, rescan the image to achieve optimum results. Notice that after the rescan the histogram shows more data in the midtones as well as cleaner whites, indicated by the expanded highlight data in the histogram.

After the rescan, touch-ups can be made in an image-editing program. In this case, I removed dust with the Rubber Stamp tool and the model's eyes were brightened with the Dodge tool.

Tip

When transparencies are scanned on flatbed scanners, light may interplay between the film and the glass platen, producing concentric rainbow-tinged rings called Newton rings in certain areas of your image. (This is why transparency scanners have no glass.) Clean up the rings on your image by bringing your scan into an image-editing program, or try a rescan after repositioning the film on a different portion of the platen.

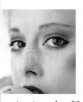

Scanning Low-Key Images

Low-key images are those with most of their data in the shadow to midtone regions. They present a challenge to flatbed scanners, which have a hard time "seeing" the dark regions of an image. The trick is to move some of the data into the midtone regions, while maintaining high contrast in the shadow regions.

The automatic "exposure" feature of most flatbed scanners has a tendency to compensate for the dark regions, resulting in washed-out scans. To get around this problem, I generally scan low-key images with no tone corrections and set black point to the darkest region of the image.

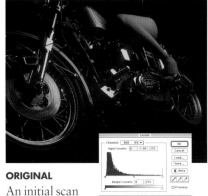

ORIGINAL
An initial scan of this 2¼" transparency shows a concentration of data in the far left portion of its histogram. Notice that very little data was picked up in the midtones and highlights of the image.

Scanning low-key images also tends to produce noise in the shadow regions. To prevent this, I suggest you scan without sharpening your image. Later on, you can select the dark regions of the image and blur them to eliminate noise, then invert the selection and sharpen the remaining midtone and highlight data.

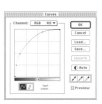

STEP 1
After bringing your initial scan into an image-editing program, adjust the overall tone by using the Curve command and adjusting the RGB channel so the image's data rises dramatically in its shadow regions. This gives you the detail you need in the dark areas of the photo.

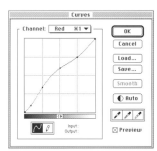

STEP 2
In this case, I also selected the red component of the curve and adjusted it to emphasize the flesh tones in the photo. Save the curve by naming it Low Key Curve or a similar identifier.

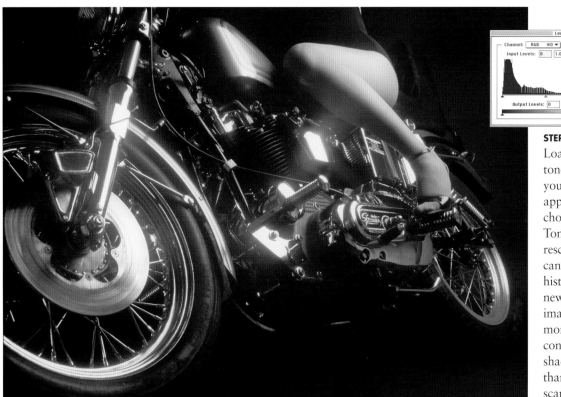

STEP 3
Load the revised tone curve into your scanning application by choosing Import Tone Curve, and rescan. As you can see from the histogram, the new scan of this image retained far more detail and contrast in the shadow regions than the original scan.

Getting the Most From a High-Contrast Original

Ah, the hardest thing to scan is a high-contrast image, unless, of course, the original image is meant to be high contrast. In that case, nothing could be easier!

But I'll assume you've turned to this demo because you have a high-contrast image on your hands that you want to make less contrasty, and that can be tricky.

The problem with a high-contrast original is that all of the data has been squished into the highlight and shadow regions with very little data left in the midtones. The job is to extract as much of the data in the shadow and highlight regions as feasible and move that data toward the middle while maintaining detail and contrast.

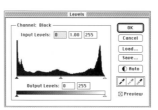

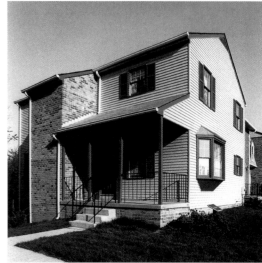

ORIGINAL
This image has highlights that are too light and shadows that are too dark. This photo was printed on high-contrast (#4) photo paper, which contributed to the problem.

A histogram of this high-contrast photo shows that the image's data is bunched at the ends of the tonal spectrum. Adjusting the Levels command won't help because it doesn't allow you to pull the data at both ends toward the middle of the spectrum.

You also might assume that the classic gamma curve is the way to go with a high-contrast original. However, using this curve results in midtones and highlights that lack detail. The only curve that works is an inverted S-curve. With this curve both the shadows and highlights are concentrated toward the midtones—just what you want.

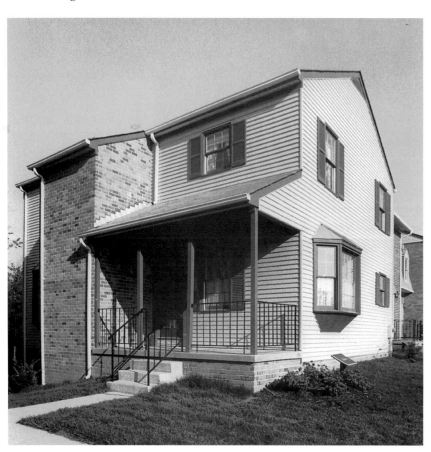

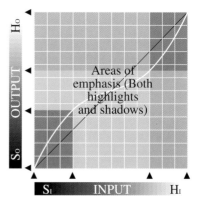

Areas of emphasis (Both highlights and shadows)

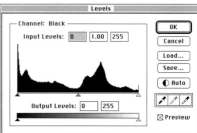

Scanning with an inverted S-curve produces an image that looks less "hot." Pulling up the histogram of this less-contrasty image confirms what the eye can see—a broader tonal range in the midtone region of the image.

Black-and-White Scans From Color

When would you ever scan in color an image intended for black-and-white reproduction? When you want to obtain better results than simply scanning in grayscale, that's when. Here's how: First, scan the image as best as it can be in color. You may want to save it for later use. For this image of yours truly, I wanted to enhance the contrast in the shirt and darken the sky. A brief check of the individual RGB channels revealed that the blue channel wasn't adding anything to the image.

In fact, other than the jacket, the data contained in the blue channel was dull as can be. Most of the data I wanted was contained in the red and green channels. (Of course, your images will have unique properties of their own.)

I started by copying the red channel to a new, empty image that had the same dimensions as the color scan. I placed the red data on the background layer. Next, I copied the green channel from the color scan and placed it on a new layer above the red. After trying various settings, I set the transparency to 60 percent, giving slightly more emphasis to the data in the green layer. Last, I merged the two layers into one (using the Merge command). The result is shown below.

This traditional grayscale scan from a color image resulted in a lack of contrast in the shirt and delivered dull gray sky. We can do better! By merging the data from the red and green layers of the color scan, you can enhance the data to obtain a better grayscale image.

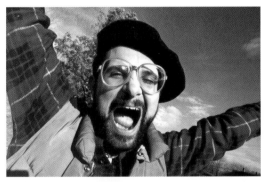

SCANNED AS GRAYSCALE

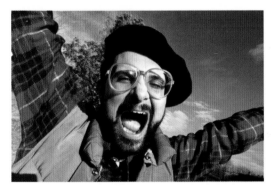

SCANNED AS COLOR

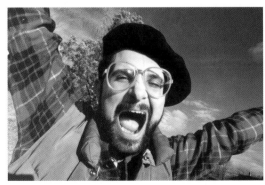

NEW IMAGE CONVERTED FROM COLOR

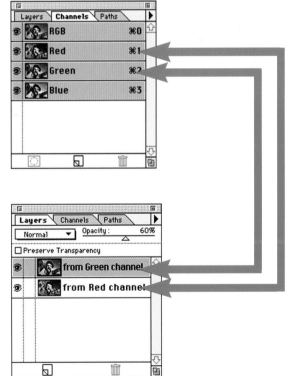

Note how much better the shirt looks—it now has the contrast needed to print well. Note that the sky is darker, too. In all, the image is vastly improved over the straight grayscale scan. The computer is the best "darkroom" I've ever owned!

Scanning Color Negatives to Make Color Positives

There's no easy way to create a color positive from a color negative with the scanning software that ships with most of today's flatbed scanners (although slide scanners are another matter). Flatbed scanner manufacturers usually (but not always) provide some tools and support for capturing transparent positives but have sorely neglected the need for information on what adjustments to make when translating a color negative into an accurate color positive.

You'll be in for a shock if you try to create a color positive by scanning a color negative as a transparency and then simply inverting it. The color of the film translates into a color positive that has a sick, bluish cast. This is because when the Invert command is applied to the scanned negative, it converts every color in the image to its complement. Because color negatives are made with an orange substrate and orange maps to blue when inverted, the results are not very appealing, to say the least.

The trick is to bring your negative image into an image-editing program, neutralize the orange cast, "invert" each of the color channels and save the final curve to use in rescanning, as shown in the following demo.

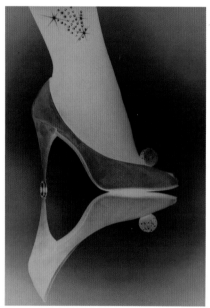 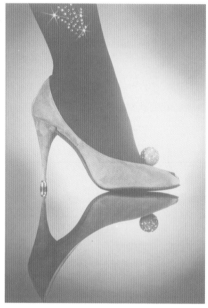 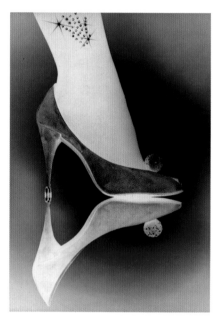

ORIGINAL
The original is a 4" x 5" color negative that was scanned as a transparency at 100 percent and 300 spi. I brought it into Photoshop and adjusted each of the color channels as shown.

WHAT NOT TO DO
Don't use the Invert command on a color negative. You'll end up looking awfully blue.

STEP 1
To neutralize the orange color cast before inverting, pull up the Adjust/ Curves/Auto feature that can be found under the Adjust Curves dialog box. Auto forces the overall color in the image to become neutral, removing the orange cast.

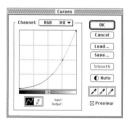

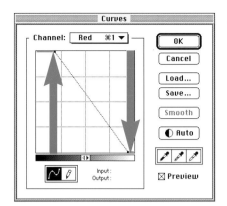

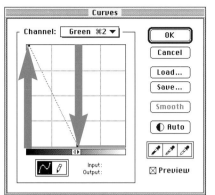

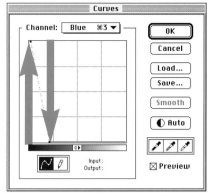

STEP 2

The image left on your screen after applying Auto is still a negative image, but you need to see what you're going to get before you rescan. To see what the positive image will be, and make any necessary adjustments, "invert" each of the color channels. Separately choose each color channel (hidden under the RGB channel menu) and invert each one by dragging the begin/end points to the exact opposite side, and voilà, a positive image!

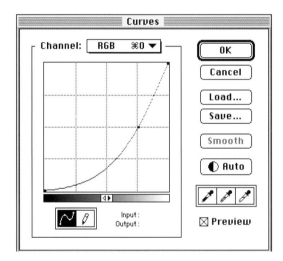

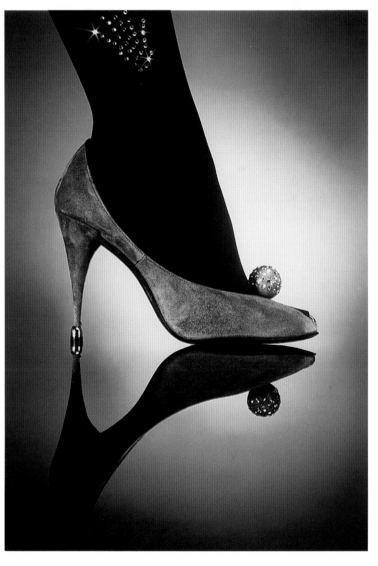

STEP 3

Go back to the RGB channel and make any overall adjustments to the tone of the image. In this case, I wanted darker midtones, so I adjusted the curve downward. If you need to make any individual color adjustments, it's best to go back to the channel in question and make minor adjustments to that particular curve (such as adjusting the red curve to the left for a warmer image).

STEP 4

Save the curve as Color Neg Curve and click OK to exit the Adjust/Curves dialog box. Rescan the image using the imported curve you just saved. You'll get a great "positive" RGB scan that you can then save, clean up and manipulate as you would any scanned image.

Creating Color Scans From a Black-and-White Scanner

As unreal as it may seem, you *can* make color images from a black-and-white scanner. Although it's somewhat time-consuming and the color isn't quite up to that of a color scanner, the quality will often do in a pinch. Here's how to do it.

You'll need to use three colored filters or gels: pure red, pure green and pure blue (not cyan). These can be purchased at office supply stores (where they're sold for overhead presentations), theatrical supply houses (where they're sold for coloring stage lights) or directly from Eastman Kodak (where they're sold for lots of money).

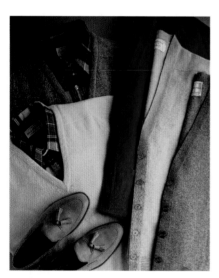

ORIGINAL

The color 4" x 5" transparency used for this demo was scanned at 300 spi for best output to four-color film at a scale of 100 percent. I taped my original to the scanning bed to prevent it from shifting each time I slipped a colored gel between it and the glass. By taping it on just one side, I could easily slip each gel between the original and the bed.

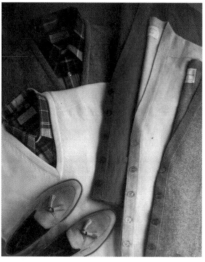

STEP 1

Slide the red gel between the original and the scanning bed. Before scanning, choose Crop and Set White Point/Set Black Point to determine the best exposure. (For this image, I chose the lightest area, the collar label on the second sweater from the right, as Set White Point and the inside of the shoe as Set Black Point.) Scan the image in grayscale mode and save it as Red Scan, or give it a similar label.

Note: The red gel is likely to be the darkest of the three colored gels, resulting in a noisy scan. You should be able to achieve a reasonable scan in spite of this if your green and blue scans are relatively noise-free.

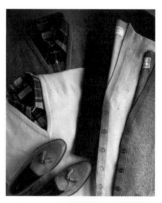

Green filter scan.

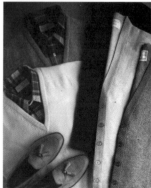

Blue filter scan.

STEP 2

Repeat this procedure for the green and blue gels, saving each file under a new name.

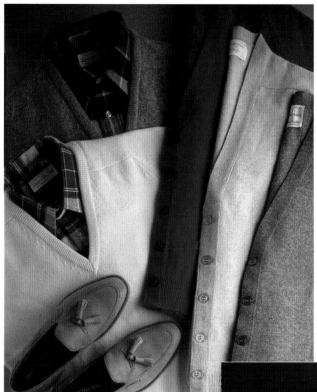

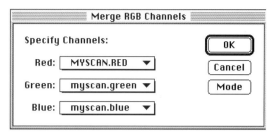

STEP 3

Combine all three grayscale scans into one RGB file by choosing Merge Channels on the Channels dialog box (under the Mode menu). Select Three-file RGB method, choose the file names and click OK. Save as Myscan RGB or a similar name, clean up and adjust as you would any other.

The color image on the left, created from a black-and-white scanner, pales in comparison with its cousin shown below, a color scan produced from a color flatbed scanner. But as a last resort, it will do.

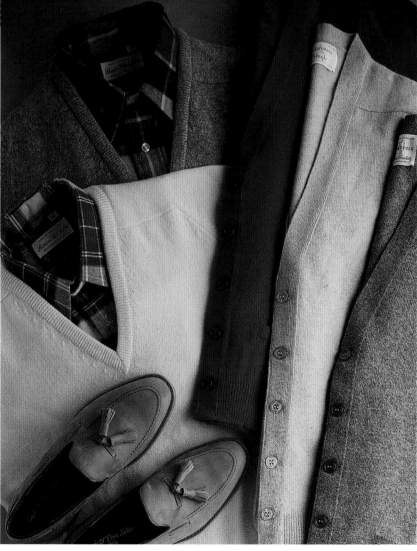

Scanning an Image Twice for Greater Range

Some images have important detail in both the shadows and highlights. Rather than use some fancy import curves (or, more important, if your scanner doesn't support such import curves), I suggest you use this technique, which involves merging the data from two separate scans—one that has been optimized to capture the highlight data and another that has been optimized to capture shadow data. Note: If your scanning software doesn't support custom import curves, choose gamma 1.8 (or higher) to capture the shadow detail.

The only thing you must be careful about is to make sure the two scans are of exactly the same image area—don't move a thing!

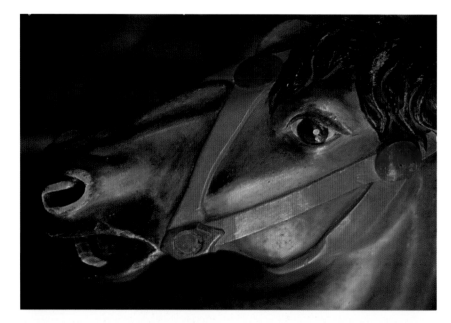

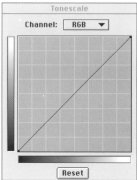

A "normal" scan of a dark slide results in the shadow data plugging up. Notice, however, the subtle yet important detail in the highlights that we want to retain. It would be nice to get better midtones as well. This is one hard-to-scan image!

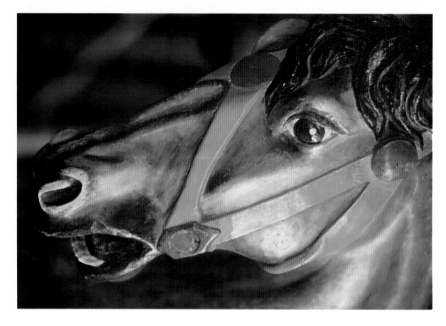

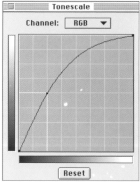

By increasing the contrast in the shadow region of the import curve we achieve much better shadows—at the expense of the highlights. Notice also the increase in contrast in the colors. By itself this scan is useless. But in combination with the above image, we can make magic.

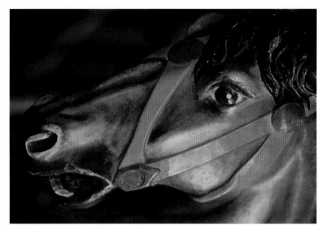

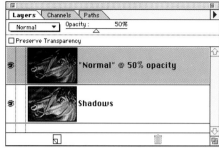

TECHNIQUE 1

Take the two scans from the previous page. Copy the shadow data on a bottom layer in Photoshop. Copy the highlight data to the top layer. Set the top layer's opacity to 50 percent. Flatten the two layers. That's it. What you'll get is a merged image composed of 50 percent highlight data and 50 percent shadow data. Many images can be improved in this manner.

The only downside to this technique is that the highlights (and colors) will tend to flatten out a bit since they are merged equally with the shadow data (which is very light indeed in the highlight region).

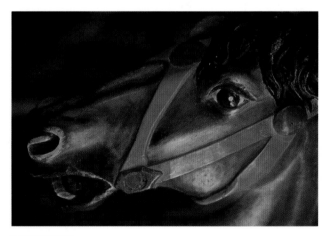

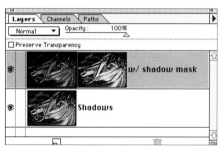

Copying the highlight data from one scan and the shadow data from another allows you to capture important data in both the highlights and the shadows.

TECHNIQUE 2

Take the two scans from the previous page. Copy the shadow data on a bottom layer in Photoshop. Copy the highlight data to the top layer. For Photoshop 3, make a copy of the shadow layer and paste it into a "mask" for the highlight layer. For Photoshop 4, paste a copy of the shadow data into a new channel and choose that channel as a selection, then immediately create a mask layer (which converts the selection data into mask data). Flatten the image and save. You're done.

The benefit of this technique is that highlight data is preserved, while the shadow data is derived mainly from the shadow layer. Midtone data is a combination of the two layers—exactly what you want.

Sharpening Scanned Images

The human eye has a natural tendency to view a scanned image as "soft" or out of focus. You'd think that a higher resolution scan would help, but that's not the case. All scanned images need some sharpening, even those scanned on high-end drum scanners. Master printers and color separators will attest to this fact—they've been dealing with this problem for years.

Unsharp masking is the trade term for a standard technique that printers and color separators use to sharpen images by accentuating the differences between adjoining areas of significantly different hue or tone. The traditional technique uses a mask that's a slightly out-of-focus duplicate of the original image. When the original is rescanned with this mask, there is an increase in the degree of contrast at the boundaries of tone shifts; however, subtle gradations in tone and hue remain untouched. The result is increased sharpness where you would normally want it—in the most highly detailed areas of the image. You can apply this same sharpening technique to your images with the Unsharp Mask filter.

AMOUNT refers to the intensity of the Unsharp Mask effect. A setting between 100 percent and 200 percent will do. My "standard" Amount setting is 120 percent; however, some images need more than this and others less. You'll need to experiment with each image.

RADIUS refers to the dimension, in width, of how much "spread" the sharpening algorithm will have.

Use too little and the image won't look sharp. Use too much and the image will have obvious "halos" around the sharpened edges. The formula to use is radius equals exactly the halftone frequency. For example, when using two times halftone frequency, use Radius 2. At 1.41 times the frequency, use Radius 1.41. For multimedia purposes use Radius 1 (no halftone multiplier). It is for this reason that I never sharpen my scans when scanning and always sharpen later in Photoshop once I have determined exactly what the final, cropped size will be.

THRESHOLD specifies the difference, in number of shades of gray, between two samples before the sharpening algorithm kicks in. In effect, it determines how many samples in an image will be sharpened. A setting of 0 will affect every sample; a setting of 50 will affect almost none of the samples. Highly detailed images, such as line art, require a setting of 3 or less, whereas portraits look best with a setting between 5 and 10. (We want to keep minor wrinkles down to a minimum, don't we?)

It can take a while to come up with the right combination of settings for an image. That's why many manufacturers of scanning software offer sharpening as an option during image capture. But I still recommend doing your own sharpening post-scan—you'll get much better results than any "automatic" solution.

Tip

Going too far with this technique yields an image that looks obviously fake. It can also produce ghostly "halos" around sharpened areas—a sure sign of too much of a good thing. Apply this technique in moderation.

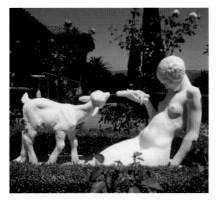

ORIGINAL

This 35mm slide with no sharpening was scanned at 1,200 spi. The overall image looks slightly (and predictably) fuzzy. The results of several different combinations of Unsharp Mask settings are shown.

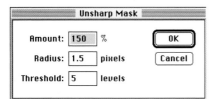

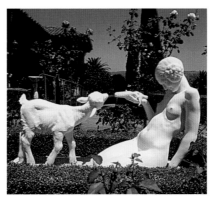

Unsharp Mask with Radius 2.0, Amount 200 percent and Threshold 1.

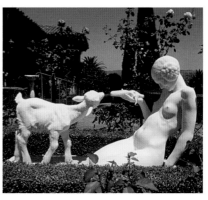

Unsharp Mask with Radius 2.0, Amount 100 percent and Threshold 1.

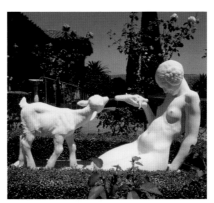

Unsharp Mask with Radius 2.0, Amount 100 percent and Threshold 5.

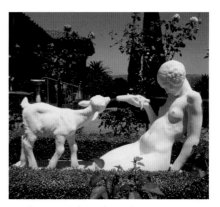

Unsharp Mask with Radius 1.0, Amount 100 percent and Threshold 5.

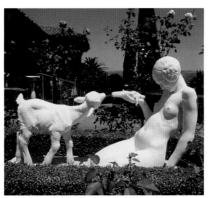

Unsharp Mask with Radius 1.0, Amount 150 percent and Threshold 5.

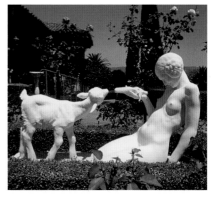

Unsharp Mask with Radius 1.5, Amount 150 percent and Threshold 5. This setting yielded the best results for output at 150 lpi.

Getting High-Res Backgrounds From Low-Res Data

Let's say you have a low-res scan that you'd like to use for a background. You need to enlarge it to fit your overall image area, but you don't want the pixelated look that results from enlarging low-res images. Well, bunky, the only way to achieve this is to fool the eye. Here's how to do it.

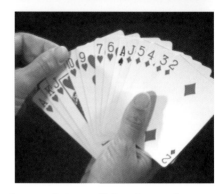

ORIGINAL
This original is a video capture—a 640 x 480 sample grayscale image shot with a black-and-white video camera. It needed to be remade into a slick, printworthy, four-color image, suitable for display on the cover of a Boston-area magazine.

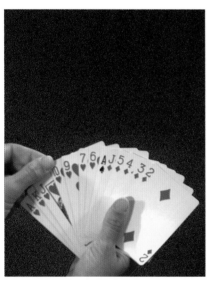

STEP 1
I captured the video signal using the software that came with my video digitizer. I then saved the image to disk in TIFF format (PICT would have worked just as well).

I opened the saved video-capture file in Photoshop. Because I wanted to add more area to the top of the image, I chose the Image/Canvas command and increased the canvas size from 640 x 480 to 640 x 960, keeping the original data confined to the bottom half of the image area.

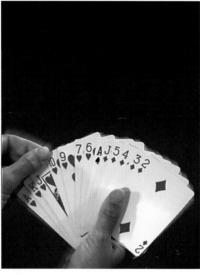

STEP 2
I converted the image from grayscale to RGB by choosing the Mode/RGB command and then enlarged it using the Image/Size command. When you enlarge, choose a resolution that is at least the minimum lpi output (for example, 150 spi), and select the proper size width of your final printed image plus allocated bleed for each dimension of at least ⅛" (0.3cm). This increases the file size of the image tremendously while the data (and apparent resolution) remains the same. That makes sense—you can't create more data where there wasn't any to begin with!

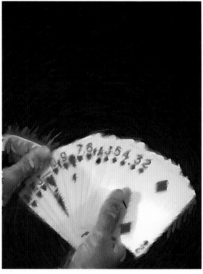

STEP 3
To fool the eye into perceiving more data than there really is, perform some painterly "magic" on the file by choosing a special effects filter. Aldus's Gallery Effects offers quite a few as does Kai's Power Tools. Some of the special effects filters supplied with Photoshop, such as the motion blur or mosaic, could work as well. For this image I chose a combination of Photoshop's radial blur and noise filters in addition to Fractal Design Painter's oil brush tool.

When the effect is complete, convert the image to a CMYK file, adjust for press conditions and dot gain, and save as a five-file EPS (also known as DCS).

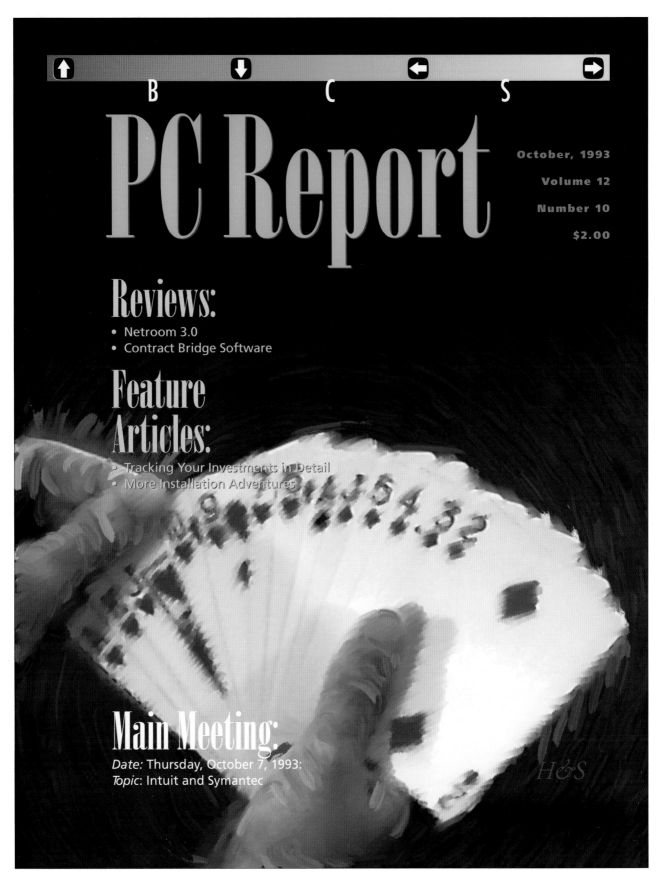

PC Report

October, 1993

Volume 12

Number 10

$2.00

Reviews:
- Netroom 3.0
- Contract Bridge Software

Feature Articles:
- Tracking Your Investments in Detail
- More Installation Adventures

Main Meeting:
Date: Thursday, October 7, 1993:
Topic: Intuit and Symantec

STEP 4   The final touch is to place something in the foreground that the eye will see first and focus on. In this case, the magazine's cover lines and logo served this purpose. The overall effect fools the observer into thinking the background contains more data than there really is. It just goes to prove the old adage: When given a lemon, make lemonade!

Getting High-Res Line Art From Low-Res Data

How do you achieve high-resolution images when you have a low-resolution scanner? You cheat! There are several ways of "cheating" or getting around the low-resolution problem. The best way depends on the type of scanner being used, the scale of your final image and how detailed your final image needs to be.

The easiest solution, by far, is to scan your image as a grayscale image instead of as line art. The 8-bit depth of a grayscale image gives the illusion of higher resolution, as compared to the 1-bit depth of a line art image.

If you own a low-res scanner, or one that won't support an 8-bit grayscale scan, you can bring the image into an image-editing program such as Photoshop and use the program's editing tools to adjust its resolution, as demonstrated in the procedure on this and the following page.

You can also use a program specifically designed to remove the bitmapped look or "jaggies" that are seen in images produced from low-res data.

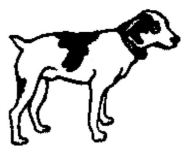

ORIGINAL
This 1-bit scan at 300 spi was made from a turn-of-the-century book of printers' and engravers' decorations.

Using Photoshop's Gaussian

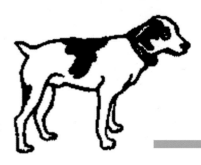

STEP 1
Convert your 1-bit line art image into an 8-bit grayscale image by bringing it into Photoshop and selecting Gray Scale from the Mode menu.

Using Ray Dream's JAG II

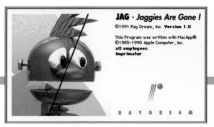

This is a one-step solution where the scanned image is opened in JAG II and the Anti-Alias command is selected. JAG II does the rest.

Scanning the Original as a

Blur and Threshold Mode

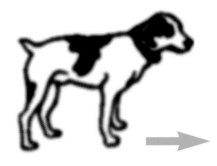

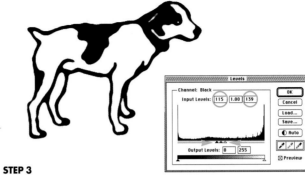

STEP 2
Apply the Gaussian Blur filter, setting the radius at 1.5 to 2.0 pixels.

STEP 3
Open the Levels dialogue box and threshold the data by moving the H_I and S_I controls toward the middle as shown. You have to experiment with each image to find out where the settings should be for optimum results.

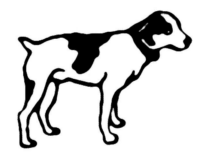

The final 300-spi image using JAG II.

Grayscale Image

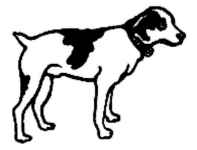

Scanning our low-res original in grayscale mode produced this 300-spi image.

Salvaging a Faded Original

I suspect this section will be one of the most read of the entire book. And the reason is obvious—there are tons of poor originals out there!

It is my firm conviction that you can obtain better images from poor negatives, prints and slides with your scanner than you can in the best photo darkroom! This is because the computer contains tools that darkroom people can only dream about. I should know—I was a professional studio photographer many years ago.

I will demonstrate how I "rescued" an old picture of my great-grandfather that I found in my parents' attic by adjusting the tonal settings on my Agfa Arcus Plus scanner before scanning, making further tonal adjustments and retouching in Photoshop. Because the final image was reproduced in four-color for this book, it was output directly from QuarkXPress separations as a set of tritone films.

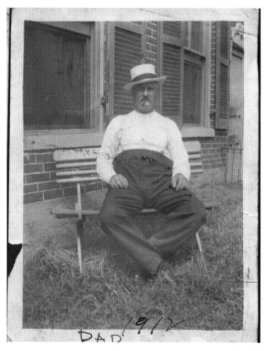

ORIGINAL

Notice how the original black-and-white photo has faded—a classic "sepia" look. This image is a good candidate for a desktop scanner since all the important data is in the midtones. Because this photo is going to be reprinted in a way that replicates its sepia-tone coloring, I will scale it at 100 percent of its original size before scanning. Scanning it at 300 spi gives me the resolution I need for output to a 150-lpi halftone screen at its original size.

It's important to make tonal corrections in a faded original by making adjustments in the lights and darks before you scan, if your scanning software allows this, and after, in an image-editing program such as Photoshop. Your goal is to enhance the tonal range of the original by deepening the shadows and brightening the highlights.

STEP 1

Preview the scan within your scanning software. Set the output levels to add depth to shadows and brighten highlights. Because Agfa's FotoLook drives my scanner, and it doesn't offer a histogram view to show the tonal range of the original, I chose to scan the original with no tone settings and then

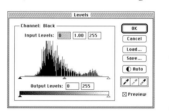

look within Photoshop at the histogram (using the Levels command) to see where the data lay. You can see how this faded image has a severely compressed tonal range.

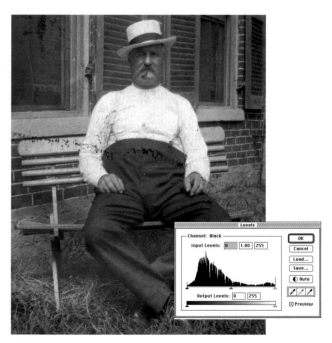

STEP 2

I selected the Dmin/Dmax command on my scanning controls to expand the tonal range of the image. The histogram of the resulting scan shows the results. I also chose to crop the original image since the background contained many stains and smudges and added nothing to the picture.

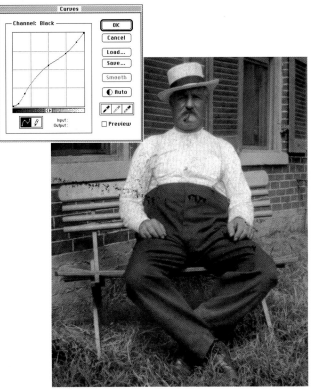

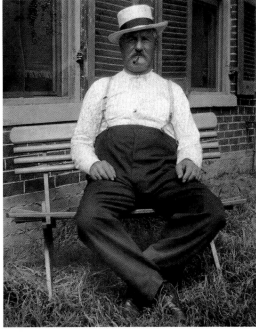

STEP 4

The only way to clean up an image like this is to get your hands dirty! I used the Rubber Stamp tool to carefully eliminate unwanted scratches, dirt and stains. I used the Burn and Dodge tool as necessary for added emphasis. In this instance, the chair, suspenders, hat and eyes were selectively darkened and/or lightened. Note: Apple's Photo-Flash software offers automated tools that make quick work of clean-up jobs such as this by eliminating scratches and dust marks. See the listing in chapter five.

STEP 3

After bringing the scanned image into Photoshop, I made further adjustments in the photo's tonal range by carefully adjusting the Curves control as shown. This adjustment added punch to the shadows and lightened the midtones without affecting the highlights.

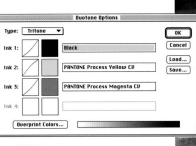

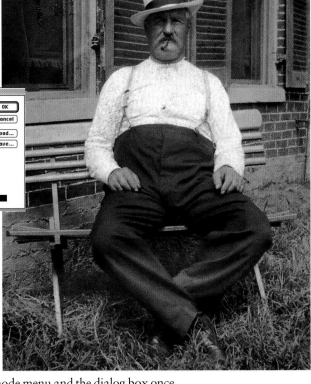

STEP 5

I chose Duotone from the Image and Mode menus in Photoshop to produce the tritone. The curves shown above for magenta, yellow and black yielded the balance I needed for each color. If you don't like the effect produced by the curves you've designated, simply choose Duotone from the mode menu and the dialog box once again appears. Select a new tone curve for each of the colors and you're back in business.

Colorizing an Old Photo

Converting an old black-and-white photo of a family member into a color version of the same photo is something your family will likely cherish (Ted Turner not withstanding). The trick is to colorize the entire photo with warm undertones to add a vintage look and then individually color different components in the photo.

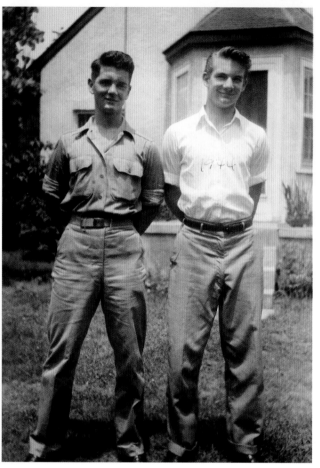

STEP 1

Bring the grayscale image into an image-editing program and convert to Duotone mode. In this case, I chose a warm reddish-brown as the second color. I adjusted the curves for this color and black as shown. When done, convert the file to RGB mode and save it under a new name.

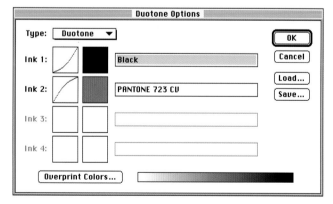

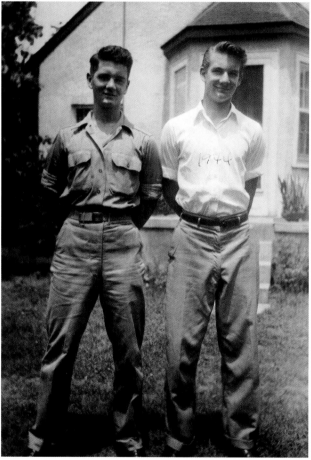

ORIGINAL

This black-and-white 8" x 10" (20.3cm x 25.4cm) photo of my dad was scanned at 200 spi as a grayscale image. I brought it into Photoshop to do the colorization.

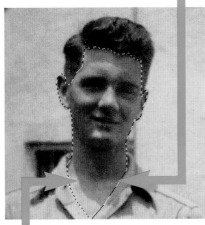

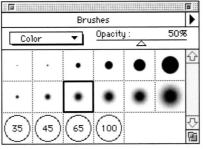

STEP 3

When using the Paintbrush in Color Mode, build up the color slowly by using an opacity of 50 percent or less.

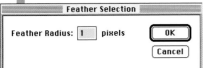

STEP 2

By isolating selected regions (defined by the marquee tool) and using the Paintbrush in Color Mode (instead of Normal), you can add whatever color you wish to your photo wherever you want it. Isolated regions should be feathered with a radius of 2.0 or more when they're selected to soften their edges.

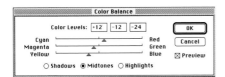

STEP 4

Individual regions can also be colorized by choosing Balance Colors, under the Image menu and Adjust submenu, and sliding the adjustments to the left (for more saturation) or right (for less) until the desired color is achieved.

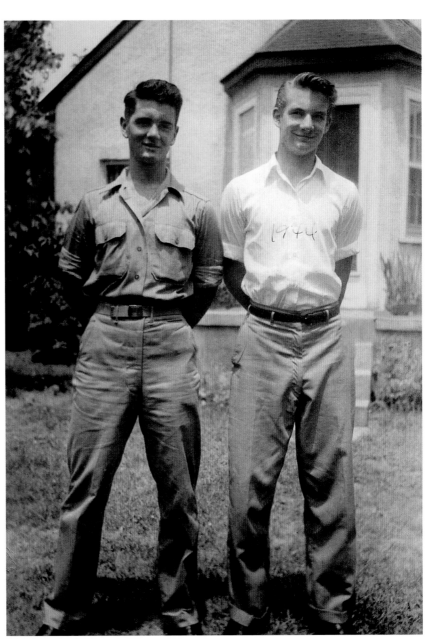

When colorizing an old photo, choose subtle colors for a realistic, timeworn look. Use a brighter, more vibrant palette for a postcardlike effect.

Reducing Scratches and Cracks

Scratches and cracks in your photos are a real pain to clean up. Flatbed scanners make the situation worse because they only light an image from one side, causing shadows and highlight artifacts. The trick is to scan the image twice—once upright and once again upside down. Bring both into Photoshop, rotate the upside-down scan 180° (to make it right side up), then merge the two images into one by pasting one image on top of the other using the Layers palette, as shown below. Make the transparency of the top image 50 percent and adjust the placement of the top image until the two images are exactly aligned. Zoom in, if necessary. Once the images are aligned, select Merge Layers and voilá—instant clean-up.

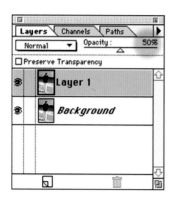

SCANNED RIGHT-SIDE UP   **SCANNED UDSIDE DOWN**

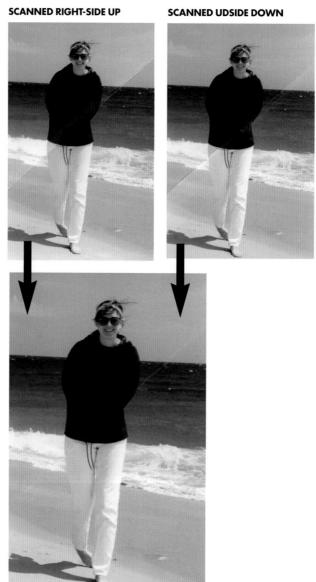

Scanning an image once right side up (above, left) and once upside down (above, right) and merging the two images cancels the highlight/shadow artifacts introduced by the scanner, making retouching much easier. The combination image of my wife, Liz, shown above, is entirely unretouched except for the use of this technique.

Scanning Thin Lines for Reduction

Scanning thin lines is pretty easy when you are scanning the original at the same size you intend to output (see Scanning Fine Line Art on page 110). The problem arises when you want to significantly reduce the image—the thin lines in your scan will print as soft shades of gray, if they print at all! This is especially true for graphics intended for the Web, where the screen resolution is inherently low (approximately 72 ppi). The solution involves using Photoshop's Minimum filter (Filter/Other/Minimum).

Scan at twice the resolution you feel is optimal for the intended output, apply the Minimum filter with Radius 1, then reduce the image size back to optimal. The difference is quite profound. Although the "normal" scan has the right tone, it has lost detail in the thinnest of lines. By scanning at twice the resolution (600 vs. 300 spi) and applying the Minimum filter, the lines all fatten up nicely. Note: In this case, applying the Minimum filter to the optimally sized image (i.e., 300 spi) would make the lines too thick, causing the shadow areas, in particular, to plug up.

Finally, save the image in the appropriate file format—GIF for the Web, TIFF for print.

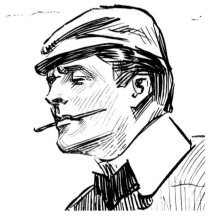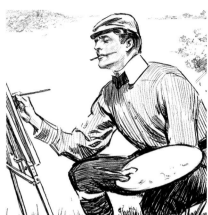

Scanned at 300 spi.

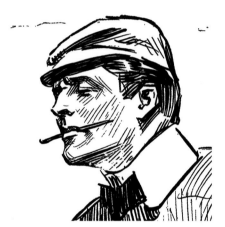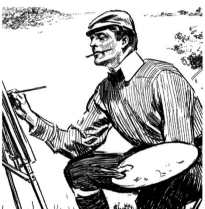

Scanned at 600 spi, Minimum filter with Radius 1, then reduced to 300 spi.

Using Photoshop's Minimum filter and scanning at twice the resolution will help save thin lines from disappearing when you reduce an image.

Scanning Fine Line Art

This highly detailed lithograph by Charles Dana Gibson can be reproduced in a variety of ways, depending on how much detail can be sacrificed for a smaller file size.

A lot depends on output. Printing it on a 300-dpi laser printer requires a less detailed image than output to film or an imagesetter. When the image goes to press, printing it on an uncoated paper requires less definition than printing it on a coated paper. A smaller image requires less definition than one that runs full page.

To hold the fine lines of this etching, one option is to scan the line art as a grayscale image. In fact, anyone with a low-resolution scanner almost always gets a better scan with grayscale than with line art mode. Why? Because resolution is affected by bit depth. The greater the bit depth, the greater the apparent resolution. This means that grayscale images, with a depth of 8 bits, always appear to have higher resolution than a 1-bit line art image. A 300-spi grayscale scan of an image should show as much detail as a 600-spi line art scan of the same image. Although the grayscale image has a lower resolution than the line art image, it has a larger file size than the line art image.

Grayscale images have other advantages over images scanned as line art. They can be manipulated and rotated more easily and are not bound by sizing considerations like a bitmapped line art image is. Bit-mapped scans can only be scaled in a page layout program by a mathematical proportion of the output frequency. Typical output resolutions of imagesetters are 1,200, 2,400 and 3,600 dpi. Thus, a 120-spi, 1-bit image imported into a page layout program should be scaled at 50 percent, 100 percent, 200 percent, 500 percent or 1,000 percent for optimal results when

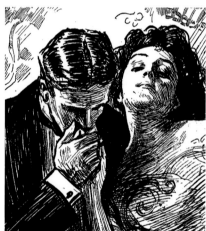

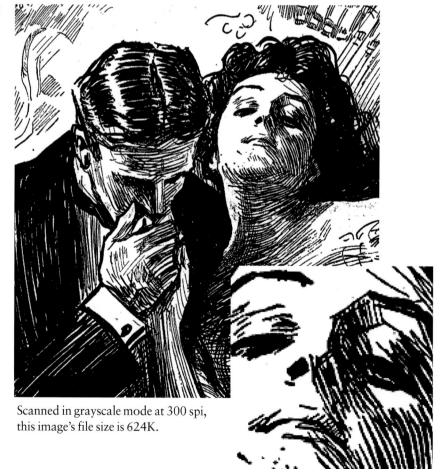

Scanned in grayscale mode at 300 spi, this image's file size is 624K.

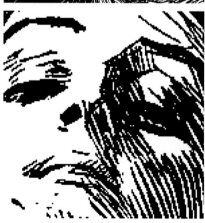

Scanned in bitmap or line art mode at 300 spi, this image's file size is 96K.

printed on a 2,400-dpi imagesetter.

The downside to using grayscale images is that they need to be halftoned at print time at typical print resolutions of 150 to 200 lpi. As a result, some types of line art images, particularly those with precise detail, may look slightly fuzzy. Line art with regular patterns may also create moirés when halftoning.

Scanning an image in line art mode may be the most appropriate choice if you're pressed for time, simply because it's usually faster to scan at this setting. Most scanners return a line art image in about half the time required for a grayscale image. This can be an important consideration if you're scanning many images at one setting.

If your scanner supports high-resolution scans, scanning at the resolution of your imagesetter's output (1,200 or even 2,400 dpi) creates the sharpest looking output

you can possibly get. 2,400-spi scans are serious stuff, but boy do they ever look good! This type of scan is used by professional publishers for high-quality art books. Remember, you can achieve an effective 2,400 spi with a 600-spi scanner simply by reducing your scan to 25 percent.

To summarize: Use grayscale for low-resolution scans of line art. For higher resolutions, 1-bit mode is best. Consult the table below.

Recommended Settings for Line Art Scanning

SCANNER MAX	IMAGESETTER	SUGGESTED SCAN MODE	SUGGESTED LINESCREEN
300 spi	300 dpi	1 bit	
600 spi	300 dpi	not recommended because of oversampling	
300 spi	600 dpi	1 bit	
600 spi	600 dpi	1 bit	
300 spi	1,200 dpi	grayscale	133
600 spi	1,200 dpi	1 bit	
1,200 spi	1,200 dpi	1 bit	
300 spi	2,400 dpi	grayscale	150
600 spi	2,400 dpi	grayscale	150
1,200 spi	2,400 dpi	1 bit	

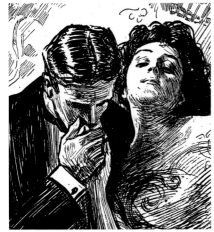

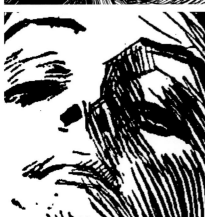

Scanned in bitmap or line art mode at 600 spi, this image's file size is 324K.

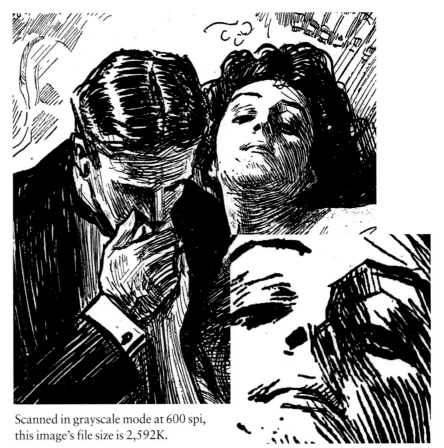

Scanned in grayscale mode at 600 spi, this image's file size is 2,592K.

Scanning Borders and Frames

CONVERSION USING PHOTOSHOP

Scanning solid black artwork to be used as a border or frame requires little other than proper alignment so that corners, vertical lines and horizontal lines are all square.

However, scanning borders that have been previously reproduced requires clean-up and conversion to suitable electronic artwork. This can be done easily with an image-editing program such as Photoshop. The final border art can then be made more workable by converting it to line art with a program such as Adobe Streamline, which converts bit-mapped artwork into editable line art.

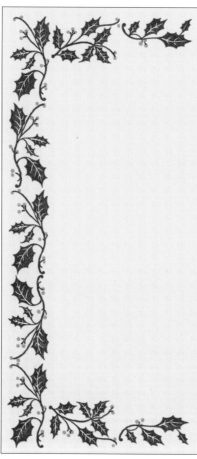

ORIGINAL

This original print came from a turn-of-the-century specifier catalog of compositors' borders and decorations. Notice in this initial scan how the paper has yellowed and the colors are muted. If your software supports it, you can eliminate the yellowed background when scanning by mapping the background color to pure white with Set White Point.

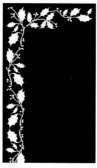

STEP 1

Bring the scan into an image-editing program. In this case, I used Photoshop. By selecting the background with the Magic Wand tool, you can isolate it from the border and create a mask.

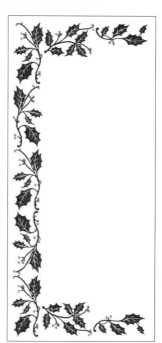

STEP 2

Create a pure white background by selecting the mask and filling it with pure white. Save this as an RGB file. For many purposes, this scan would do just fine as is, but because I wanted a "spot" color version for use in a design I was creating in PageMaker, I took this version of the border through additional steps as depicted.

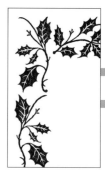

#2 Red Channel

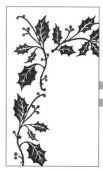

#2 Green Channel

#2 Blue Channel

STEP 3

I created an electronic mechanical or spot color version of the border by using the channel calculation commands under the Image menu. In this case I (a) duplicated the red channel, (b) calculated the difference between the red and green channels and inverted the results to obtain the red berries and (c) duplicated the green channel and moved it into the blue channel.

Calculate/
Duplicate

#3 Red Channel

Calculate/
Difference
and invert

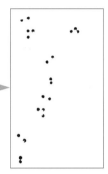

#3 Green Channel

Calculate/
Duplicate

#3 Blue Channel

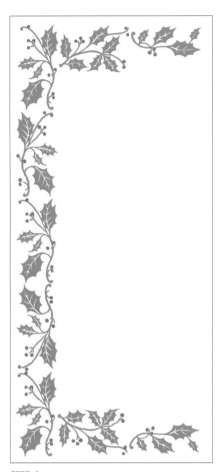

STEP 4
Because I wanted a mechanical made up of solid art, I used the Levels command to eliminate any "grayness" in the final border.

Conversion Using Adobe Streamline

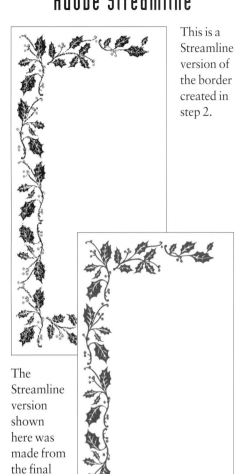

This is a Streamline version of the border created in step 2.

The Streamline version shown here was made from the final electronic mechanical shown in step 4.

The electronic mechanical created with Photoshop works, but it's an incredibly large file, weighing in at 4.2MB—and that's just half of a complete border!

Adobe Streamline converts color images into line art, resulting in a smaller file size, which in turn means faster printing and more flexibility when incorporating your scanned border into other art.

Using Streamline couldn't be easier. Import the image into the program, set a few controls to tell Streamline what kind of conversion you want (outline or inline, color or black and white, tight or loose tolerance, etc.). In a short time you have Adobe Illustrator compatible line art. Save the file to disk and you're done.

Scanning Postal Codes and Signatures

An electronic file of postal codes can be a real time-saver for desktop publishers wanting to imprint their envelopes and postcards with this information. The U.S. Postal Service makes it relatively easy for you to acquire the art you need as your original for scanning.

First, apply for a business reply mail (BRM) or business reply card (BRC) permit from the USPS. A few business days later, you will receive a printout or hard copy original with the Facing Identification Mark (FIM) and the POSTNET bar code for your particular zip code as well as the postage indicia or permit imprint that goes where the stamp is normally affixed.

Before the days of desktop publishing, this printout was pasted down as a traditional mechanical that was then taken to a printer for printing. However, you can use your scanner to incorporate this artwork into as many electronic mechanicals as you wish. The trick is to be sure your scan is perfectly square and that there is no variation in the width of the bars.

You'll want to scan these items as a single piece of artwork, just as the USPS furnishes them, with the alignment guides intact. Although this results in a larger file, it aids greatly in the placement of your scan in a page layout program.

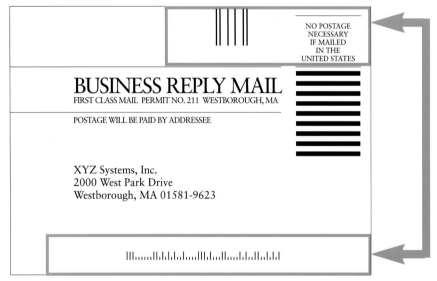

Scan these regions from the Post Office art in their entirety (as shown) to assist with accurate placement in your mechanicals.

BAR CODES

For artwork such as this, where accuracy and crispness are of prime importance, high-resolution 1-bit scanning in line art mode works best. Grayscale scans tend to be too fuzzy. Scan at a resolution of 600 spi or higher to capture the artwork. You may have to rescan and adjust the original several times to be sure the artwork is perfectly square.

Whether it's a postcard or an envelope, I suggest you take a laser print of the final artwork to your local U.S. Post Office and have them OK the layout. They should be able to test the bar codes and FIM on their equipment to make sure they can be accurately read.

Tip

I suggest you avoid using previously printed artwork as an original. You can pick up debris and texture from the paper when you scan, necessitating post-scan clean-up. The printing process also may have resulted in smeared ink or distortions, such as shearing the angle of the bar code or FIM.

You're also taking a chance of not meeting postal regulations when you copy a non-USPS original—possibly an illegitimate one. It's just not worth taking a chance—get a USPS-approved original.

Signatures

If you send a lot of faxes, having your signature on hand to place into your documents can be a real time-saver. Scan your signature at an spi that is a multiple of your output device. For instance, if your fax machine outputs images at 200 dpi, you want to scan your signature at 200 spi. Save it as a TIFF file, and it's ready to import into a page layout or word processing program.

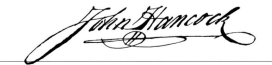

Using a Polaroid Camera With a Scanner

If you're in a pinch for a quick image, Polaroid offers an instant solution. Take a picture of your subject with a Polaroid camera, scan the picture into your computer and voilà—you've captured your image! Polaroid's new professional Polacolor PRO 100 instant print film is extremely accurate and provides highly detailed results. However, be careful when using Polaroid black-and-white instant film—it requires a special liquid coating to prevent the image from deteriorating. Give this coating plenty of time to dry before you put the image down on the glass platen—it's very sticky and hard to remove!

For more information on tone correcting, see chapter one, page 15.

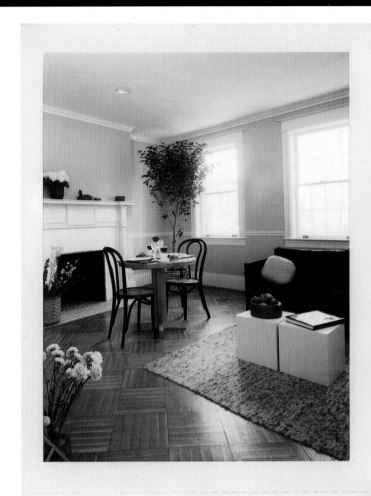

ORIGINAL
Take your picture, remembering to keep the exposure even, the camera steady and subject(s) in focus. Compose the subject matter to completely fill the image area of the film to minimize the need for cropping when you scan. This particular print was made using Polacolor type 59 instant print film, a standard for "everyday" use with a 4" x 5" camera. After making sure your print is completely dry, place it on the glass platen of your scanner.

Scan at 300 spi at 100 percent—about the maximum resolution limit of Polacolor instant print film. This 200 percent enlargement of my original 1:1 scan shows that the detail available in a Polacolor print is quite good. I have even used Polacolor prints for full-bleed 8½" x 11" (21.6cm x 27.9cm) backgrounds!

If necessary, bring the completed scan into an image-editing program and tone correct as you would for any other scanned image.

Creating Custom Computer Screens

CREATING A MACINTOSH STARTUP SCREEN

People like to customize their computers. Especially if it doesn't cost anything! Nothing could be easier. Follow these instructions to create a custom screen that will appear every time you start up your Macintosh. A bonus is that this method doesn't use up any precious system memory since a startup screen is flushed from memory once the system boots.

Scan your original to exact screen size or larger than intended screen size (see table in step 1 below).

Macintosh 12" Display	512 x 384 pixels
Macintosh 13" & 14" Display	640 x 480 pixels
Macintosh 17" Display	832 x 624 pixels
Macintosh 20" Display	1,024 x 768 pixels

STEP 1

Crop and resize in Photoshop to achieve the correct pixel dimensions. Use these measurements for standard display monitors with 8-bit color.

STEP 2

Convert to Index Color Mode/8-Bit System Palette with dither. Then choose the Save As command from the File menu.

Nearly any kind of original will do since the computer's screen resolution is significantly smaller than what is typically used for print. For my startup screen I used a 4" x 5" snapshot of my daughter with her cousin. I scanned it in at 300 spi and scaled it to cover an area of 1,200 x 1,500 pixels—big enough to fill even the largest computer screen. Once you've scanned your image, clean up and color-correct in an image-editing program, if necessary.

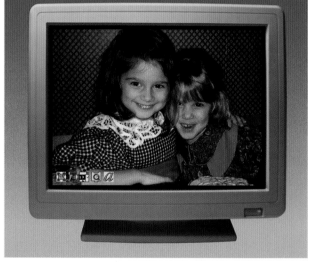

STEP 3

Name the file "StartupScreen" and choose PICT Resource as the File Format. Save the file StartupScreen in your system folder, and that's it! The next time you boot your machine, you will see the startup screen image displayed. Most people are impressed when they see a picture of your loved ones lighting up the screen at startup. Needless to say, it can remind you what's really important in life.

CREATING A MACINTOSH COMPUTER SCREEN BACKGROUND

It's easy to create a custom background screen for your Macintosh. But before you begin, you'll need to purchase a control panel/INIT such as DeskPicture from Now Utilities to load the background onto your computer. Once that's taken care of the rest is simple.

I used the same photograph of my daughter and her cousin to create a custom background screen for my Macintosh in the following demo.

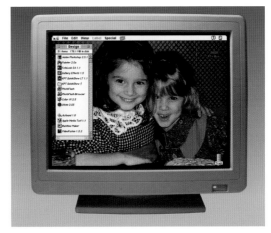

STEP 1

Before you begin, take note of the amount of memory a background screen will take up in your system folder. Here's the amount of memory required for the following screen sizes:

Macintosh 12" Display	196K
Macintosh 13" & 14" Display	307K
Macintosh 17" Display	519K
Macintosh 20" Display	786K

STEP 2

Follow steps 1 and 2 for Creating a Macintosh Startup Screen, except when sizing for your screen, subtract 20 pixels from the height of the image to allow room for the Macintosh menu bar and save the image as a PICT file instead of PICT Resource. Name this file anything you want, but be sure to check your application to see if special names are required.

Install and launch the control panel/INIT to load the picture into memory. Reboot your Mac to see your new background.

CREATING A WINDOWS 3.1 SCREEN BACKGROUND

The same kind of custom background screen can easily be achieved on a PC. You need to scan the original to exact size or larger than the intended screen size and color-correct as necessary in an image-editing program as described in the Macintosh version of creating a startup screen. This method does take up some system memory, so take heed.

13" VGA Display	640 x 480 pixels	307K
16" Super VGA Display	800 x 600 pixels	480K
19" Super VGA Display	1,024 x 768 pixels	786K

STEP 1

If your screen background image is too large to fit on screen or if it doesn't fit in memory, Windows won't load it. Check this chart showing the amount of system memory required to handle an 8-bit color image to be sure your PC can handle the image you want to load on your screen.

STEP 2

Crop and resize in Photoshop to achieve correct pixel dimensions for your particular screen. Convert to Index Color Mode/8-Bit System Palette with dither. Choose the Save As command from the File menu and name this file Myfile.BMP or any other legal DOS name. Choose File Format: BMP and save in the C:\Windows subdirectory.

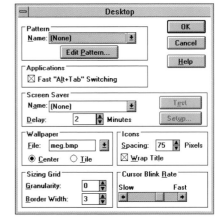

STEP 3

Open the Control Panel in the main program group and choose the Desktop icon.

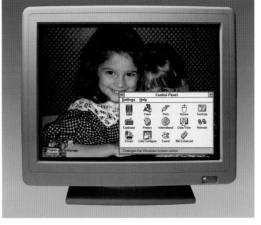

STEP 4

Select your BMP file from the Wallpaper File list box and check Center. Reboot Windows to see your screen background.

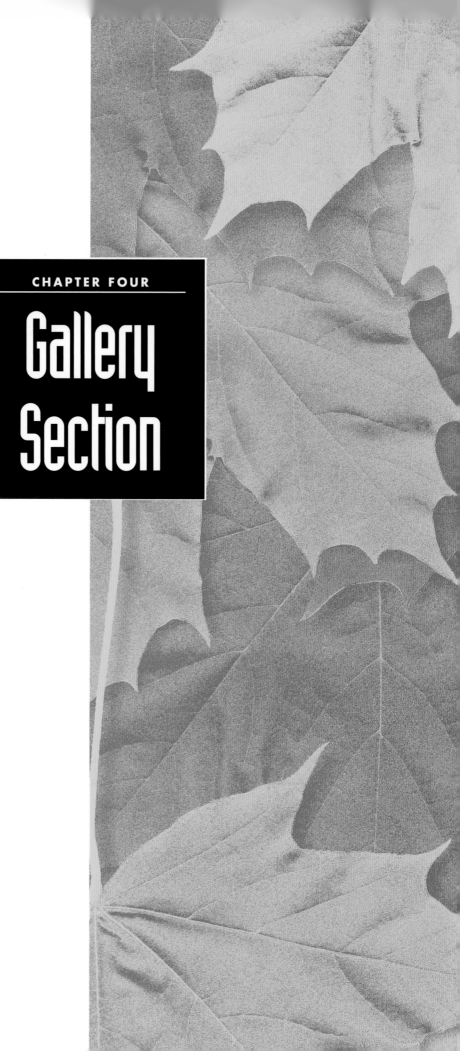

CHAPTER FOUR

Gallery Section

Introduction

Most of us in the graphic arts rely on our studio scanners for bringing all kinds of visuals into the publications and promotions we produce. Scanners have become our studio workhorses, saving time and money by replacing conventional photostats, separations and halftones that would have otherwise been produced by outside vendors. Our scanners are in constant use, capturing photos, illustrations, logos and other graphic elements, but most of us rarely take the time to fully explore our scanner's capacity for more creative applications.

Some of our more adventurous colleagues, however, have been experimenting with scanners as an artistic medium, developing innovative techniques that go far beyond the traditional pre-press graphics and image digitizing most of us do. These creative professionals are using their scanners to produce exciting visual effects not possible with conventional photography or prepress technology.

Some are using scanners to salvage treasured photographs, restoring them to gallery-worthy status with state-of-the-art hardware and their own custom software. Others have found they can use their scanner much like a studio camera, capturing models and other subjects with dramatic results that exceed the capability of traditional photographic methods. Even more are experimenting with collage effects, achieving a sense of incredible depth and realism by scanning arrangements of objects placed directly on the scanning bed. Each of these individuals has interjected his or her own artistic vision into the scanning process to produce a variety of exciting results.

This chapter features the work of these creative professionals and shows how state-of-the-art scanning technology has been fully exploited in the development of some of the most unique imagery to be seen in years. We've chosen to focus on six creative teams and individuals who have elevated scanning to an artform, producing outstanding work that has received recognition from both the design and fine arts communities. Much of it has won awards, been featured in design annuals or even appeared in museum collections.

These individuals have explored and refined their scanning methods through trial and error and countless hours of experimentation. They will share some of their techniques and scanning tips with you in this chapter. I am pleased to showcase their work in this section as well as the story behind each piece featured in the hope that you will be as amazed and inspired as I am by the creative potential inherent in scanning as a new artistic medium.

ArtScans

David Coons is a color specialist who, with his wife Susan, runs a large-format scanning service for computer and fine artists. ArtScans offers true four-color reproduction through direct digitization of large-scale art on a custom-built scanner for which they wrote the software. Many fine artists prefer their scanner over conventional, high-end drum scanners for its purity—it eliminates the need to scan from a transparency of the art.

Based just outside Los Angeles, in Manhattan Beach, California, Coons also writes specialized in-house color management software used to customize reproduction quality for their printing clients. Both he and Susan have a great appreciation for art and photography, and enjoy the challenge of faithfully reproducing fine art.

While working for Walt Disney's Feature Animation department in 1989, Coons was introduced to photographer/musician Graham Nash (of Crosby, Stills and Nash) by a mutual friend, Steve Boulter, of Iris Graphics, Inc. Nash had accumulated a library of stunning photographs of fellow musicians over the course of his remarkable career. When he learned of Coons's extensive knowledge in four-color reproduction, Nash supported him in the resurrection of a number of these prints. Among the prints Nash and Coons worked to make gallery-worthy was a portrait of David Crosby taken early in the musician's career. Nash had a 2" x 2½" (5.1cm x 6.4cm) contact sheet proof of the portrait, but nothing else to work with—the negative and original print were long since gone.

In addition to scanning the Crosby image as a substantial, one-step enlargement, Coons needed to retain detail and richness in the midtones and shadows of the

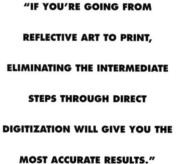

"IF YOU'RE GOING FROM REFLECTIVE ART TO PRINT, ELIMINATING THE INTERMEDIATE STEPS THROUGH DIRECT DIGITIZATION WILL GIVE YOU THE MOST ACCURATE RESULTS."

portrait. Coons did a number of experimental scans, working on several flatbed scanners and using off-the-shelf software, but he decided that the job warranted the development of a custom application. Working on a NeXT computer, which has a UNIX-based platform, Coons developed a remarkable program that utilizes all four colors in the reproduction of black-and-white prints. The highlights and lighter midtones of the Crosby portrait are all composed of black. However, when the midtones reach the point where the grays are 50 percent black, the remaining inks (cyan, magenta and yellow) are gradually eased in to add richness to the darker grays of the shadow regions. The solid black areas are made up of a 100 percent saturation of all four colors.

The Crosby scan was reproduced by making an Iris print on 100 percent rag, Arches cold-press watercolor paper. The rich texture and deckled edge of the paper add to the portrait's sense of depth and intimacy.

Nash, Coons and Boulter subsequently formed Nash Editions, a professional digital printmaking studio. They brought in Mac Holbert (CSN's former road show manager) to run the company, and Jack Duganne (a professional fine art printing specialist) to fine tune the process. Coons and his wife have since founded ArtScans, and digitize fine art originals for Nash and many other Giclée and fine art lithography printing companies around the country.

David Coons • ArtScans • 1145 Oak Ave. • Manhattan Beach, CA 90266 • Phone: (310) 545-2356 • E-mail: Dave@artscans.com

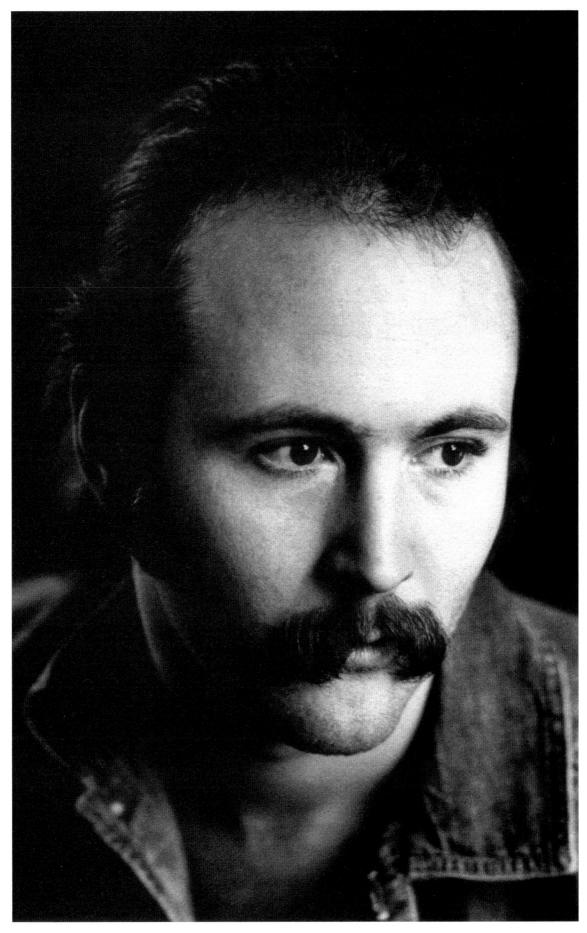

Darryl Curran

Darryl Curran is chairman of the art department and teacher of photography at California State University Fullerton. He has worked with photographic imagery and light-sensitive processes for the past thirty years and recently expanded into using the scanner as a "camera" to capture images for photomontages.

Unlike most computer artists, who scan images and then arrange them within an image-editing program, Curran composes his photomontages directly on the scanning bed. He uses the term *scanograms* to describe this medium. His prints have an unusual sense of depth and are quickly gaining recognition in the fine arts community. In fact, several are now in the collection of the Los Angeles County Museum of Art.

A self-confessed "pack rat," Curran starts a photomontage by bringing boxes of found items to Nash Editions, a Southern California-based fine art and digital printmaker. Curran rents time on the studio's Agfa Arcus scanner, together with Photoshop.

Curran's collection of objects ranges from scraps of fabric to garden tools to things found on the roadside. He arranges them directly on the scanning bed, layering objects so that the first items on the bed are in the foreground. Curran prefers to work this way because the scanner's illumination provides a unique sense of depth, unobtainable through arranging individually scanned objects. Objects in the foreground have a remarkable degree of detail, while those in the background appear soft and dark, eventually fading into oblivion.

Curran usually spends two to three hours producing anywhere from two to six photomontages, working with Mac Holbert, cofounder and operations manager of Nash Editions, and Ruthanne Holbert, imaging special-

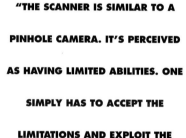

"THE SCANNER IS SIMILAR TO A PINHOLE CAMERA. IT'S PERCEIVED AS HAVING LIMITED ABILITIES. ONE SIMPLY HAS TO ACCEPT THE LIMITATIONS AND EXPLOIT THE SCANNER'S UNTAPPED POTENTIAL."

ist. Curran makes adjustments, arranging and rearranging his objects after viewing his composition in preview mode, until he has the scan he wants.

Before the final scan is made, he makes color alterations by adjusting the Gamma. All other settings are left on auto. Final scans are now made at 600-spi resolution, resulting in a file size of approximately 80MB, for output up to a 32" x 46" (81.3cm x 116.8cm) Iris Ink Jet print.

Nash Editions prints Curran's photomontages on Rives BFK 100 percent rag, a French handmade paper normally used for watercolor and printmaking.

The two images on the following page were assembled in the manner described above. *Welcome* was an old silkscreen that Curran had printed years ago and hadn't had the heart to throw away. Curran thought that it might be a good topic (welcome to Bethlehem) and a chance to backlight something on a scanner. He combined the papaya and bound grasses with the silkscreen, backlit with a halogen desk lamp and scanned with the scanner's lamp, too.

Teacup was something else. The round bowl at the top didn't work, so he lifted it up slightly and lit it from the side with a desk lamp. As you can see, the lamplight records as orange, which works well visually in this case.

Curran has sold a number of his scanned montages to fine art collectors. Because Nash Editions keeps his scanned images on file, there's no need for Curran to archive an edition of prints. As for the future, Curran has in mind a series of large-scale diptychs and triptychs.

Darryl Curran • Art Department Chairman • California State University Fullerton • Attn: Art Department • P.O. Box 34080 • Fullerton, CA 92634-9480 • Phone: (714) 278-3471 • E-mail: dcurran@fullerton.edu

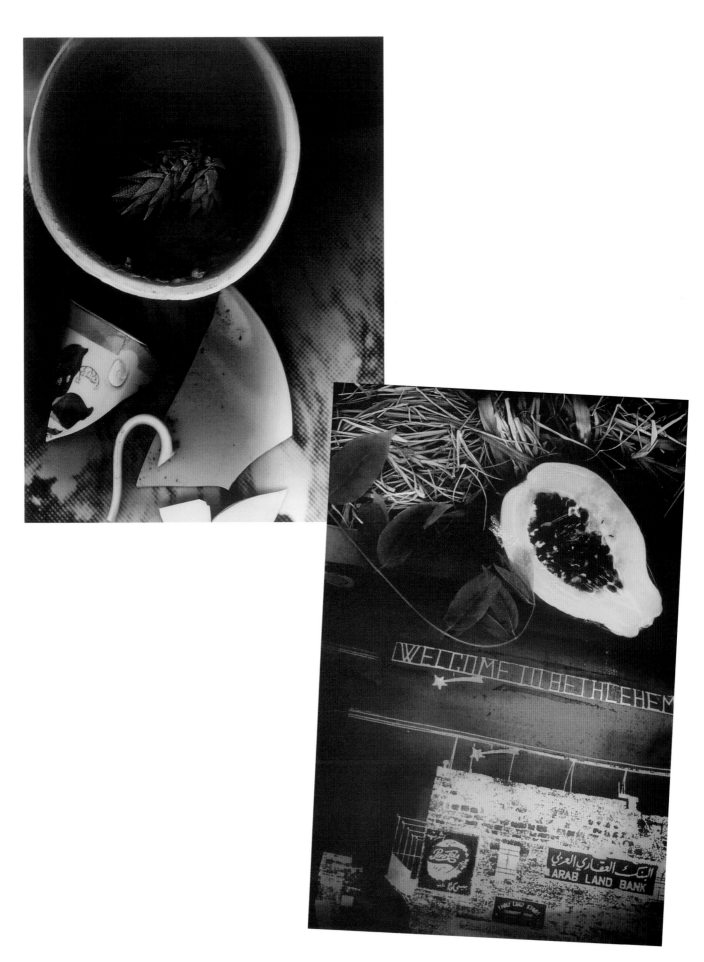

Katrin Eismann

Katrin Eismann has an enviable job for an artist: Hired as a consultant for clients such as Eastman Kodak Company, Adobe Systems and Apple Computer, she travels around the world to lecture, teach, evangelize and demonstrate the latest imaging technology to professional photographers, commercial labs and educators. Although her schedule is very full, she finds time to photograph and experiment with her own artwork.

The funny thing is, Eismann practically stumbled into this career. While a photography major at RIT (Rochester Institute of Technology) in the late eighties, she decided that the darkroom, with its chemicals and environmental problems, was not a place she wanted to spend a lot of time in. When an opportunity came to take digital imaging classes from Professor Douglas Ford Rea, she jumped at the chance and hasn't looked back since.

Eismann's techniques challenge the rules of traditional photography. Currently, she makes unorthodox use of scanners and digital cameras to create new images that investigate cultural stereotypes and media icons. Eismann's most important body of work addresses the relationship of gender, media, body image and self-esteem from her perspective as a woman and first-generation American.

To create images, Eismann combines photography, painterly techniques and scans of three-dimensional objects. Working with the computer allows her both tremendous control and a creative opportunity that is not limited to working with a single medium. The ability to combine painting, photography, textures and found objects enables her to freely experiment and explore a variety of stylizations and messages.

> **"THE FASCINATING THING ABOUT MAKING DIRECT SCANS IS THE COMBINATION OF INCREDIBLE CONTROL, FLEXIBILITY AND NEAR-INSTANT FEEDBACK THAT MADE WORKING DIGITALLY EXCITING AND INSPIRING IN THE FIRST PLACE. "**

Oil Paints, (facing page, bottom) is one of the first digital images Eismann did. Using an older model three-pass scanner, she moved the tubes of paint while the scanner made its three passes, resulting in subtle "ghostlike" images in each of the three color channels. Another of her hallmarks is the use of clear acetate to protect the glass platen, which allows her to pour paint onto the scanner's surface.

Glasses (facing page, middle) was done while Eismann was employed by the now-closed Kodak Center for Creative Imaging in Camden, Maine. While the scanner was scanning, she rolled the glasses down the platen, creating interesting distortion and colors in the glasses. The final prints were printed with the Kodak 7700 thermal dye sublimation printer.

Waterbabies (facing page, top) is a newer piece. By modifying her UMAX PowerLook II's inside lid to be covered in "blue screen" blue paper and utilizing Ultimatte blue screen software, Eismann can quickly silhouette any object placed on her scanner. The plastic fish and the doll's head pieces shown are an example of this technique. Combining these scans of objects with scans from 2¼" chromes, she layers her art and combines it in different ways until it feels "just right." The final image was output on a Durst Lambda 130 Laser LED printer at 30" x 30" (76.2cm x 76.2cm) and 200 spi.

Eismann is currently working an a book for Hayden Press, *Digital Photography: Digital Tools for the Modern Photographer*, to be published in the fall of 1997.

Katrin Eismann • PRAXIS Digital Solutions • 3400 Ben Lomond Place, #218 • Los Angeles, CA 90027 • Phone: (213) 663-5626 • Fax: (213) 663-5626 • E-mail: praxis1@earthlink.net

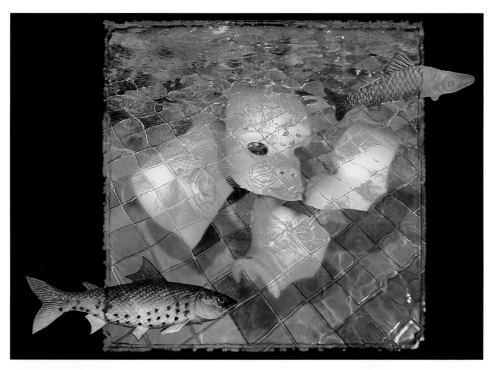

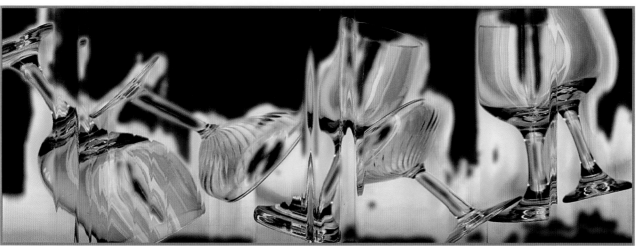

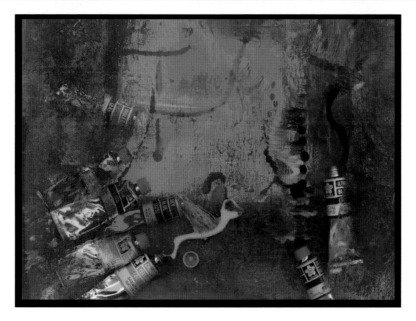

Eric Dinyer

Lost souls, trapped spirits and tortured textures blend together in the artwork of Eric Dinyer. Rarely has an artist captured such a unique and gut-wrenching vision from head to hand and into technology. And don't think that you have to play the starving artist to be true to your innermost demons. Dinyer's successful and expanding career includes commissioned work by Time Warner Books, TVT/WaxTrax! Records (including the *Black Box* and *Chainsuck* releases) and magazines such as *Newsweek*, *Ray Gun* and *Psychology Today*. If that isn't enough, the prolific Dinyer has ambitious plans of his own for 1997: a print and multimedia project entitled Luminaria and the birth of Dreamless Studios.

Early in his career, Dinyer took to a philosophical view of art. "I had an incredible art history professor, Norris K. Smith, who absolutely made me fall in love with the meaning and making of images. Professor Smith would speak so beautifully and philosophically about Rembrandt's work, that his words still resonate with me today."

Other influences include the Austro-German poet Rainer Maria Rilke. Rilke's *Duino Elegies* characterizes death as a transformation of life into an invisible inner reality that, together with life, forms a unified whole—a concept Dinyer embraces. He believes this is how he unconsciously uses the human form in his work. As you can see from the images on the following page, Dinyer uses the human form in a very sculptural or elusive manner, yet always in a gritty or distorted way.

With more commissioned work than he knows what to do with, Dinyer has never suffered from the classic "fine artist vs. commercial artist" syndrome. Photographer, illustrator, new media artist—call him whatever you like. It doesn't really matter, because he has enormous creative freedom and enjoys what he does.

Dinyer has always had a thing for roadkill. When designer Carlos Segura contacted him about doing the *Afterburn* CD cover, he needed to find a texture that looked burned. He had his eye on a squirrel, which, sadly, had been run over on the street in front of his house, but he didn't have the nerve to photograph it because he thought his neighbors would think he was crazy.

The next day, Dinyer walked out on his back patio and found a squirrel that had been impaled by something—he took it as a sign from above! He got out his shovel and moved the unfortunate critter next to his air conditioner. That evening a neighbor cat came and disemboweled the little fella. The next day he brought the squirrel in and laid him directly on his Microtek III flatbed and scanned away.

The main texture, which appears to be burned skin, is the scanned squirrel guts composted over a photograph of Dinyer. The client loved the final images and package design.

> "I'M VERY AGGRESSIVE WITH MY SCANNERS. I RECENTLY BROKE ONE BY LYING ON IT! I TREAT SCANNERS LIKE THEY'RE A CROSS BETWEEN A CAMERA AND A CANVAS. I COMPOSE DIRECTLY ON THE SCANNER BY LAYING OBJECTS DIRECTLY ON THE FLATBED, THEN SCAN, THEN REARRANGE BASED ON THE SCAN. I'VE ALSO PAINTED DIRECTLY ON THE SCANNER GLASS, DUMPED ASH TRAYS, COFFEE AND TURPENTINE ON IT AND BASICALLY TREAT SCANNERS LIKE ARTISTIC TRASH CANS!"

Eric Dinyer • 8975 Cedar Dr. • Shawnee Mission, KS 66207 • Phone: (913) 642-6607 • Fax: (913) 642-5006 • E-mail: dinyr@gvi.net

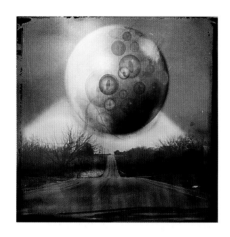

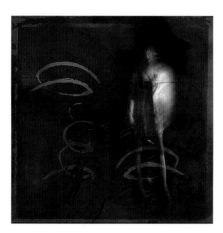

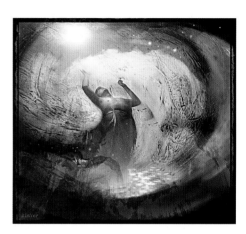

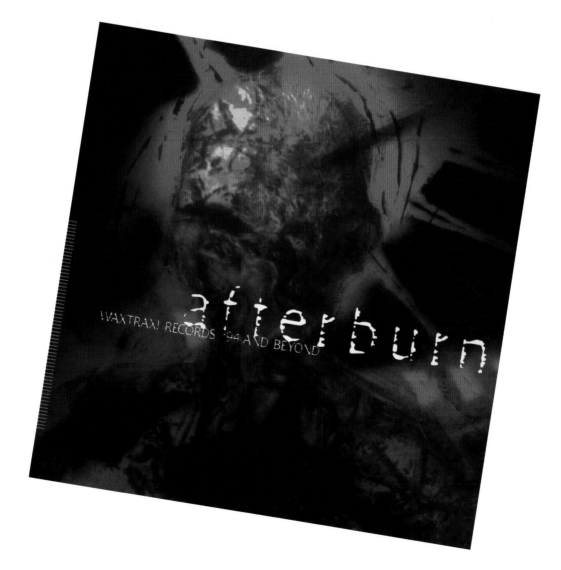

NancyScans, Inc.

Nancy Olson of NancyScans has found a way to incorporate her business and her lifestyle. With her husband, infant son and a handful of dedicated employees, she operates her custom scanning service in a rural farming community two hours from New York City.

When Olson launched her business in 1994 she had some unique goals: to do good custom scans for an appreciative clientele, to avoid the headaches of big-city business and to live in the country where the air is clean.

She describes a typical custom-scan client: "Many of our clients are photographers who have spent considerable time making the perfect black-and-white print for scanning, but scanning black and white can be tricky. The coal miner image on the following page is a good example. The original image looked great—for a gallery wall—but for scanning purposes there were problems. It had an extreme range from highlight to shadow, but while it offered detail in the shadow, the detail was within a narrow range of its own. Much of the beauty of the image was created by the detail within this slight range. To complicate matters, the print was printed on a fiber-base paper. Today's high-end scanners are so capable that they can capture detail right down to the fiber. This fiber translates as white spots or dust. You can filter it out, but in doing so you lose so much sharpness that it's not a viable solution."

Olson first mounted the 35mm negative under oil and mylar to minimize the presence of grain that would be enhanced by this considerable magnification. After doing the first prescan, she set her black point and white point to allow the maximum amount of detail to be captured. These settings produced a scan that looked far different than the original fiber-base print she was asked to match. The file Olson had created was intentionally much flatter and showed little of the drama of the original, but it was perfect for the next step in the scanning process—"color" correction.

After scanning the black-and-white image in color, Olson transferred the CMYK image from her capture system onto her cleanup station (a Power Computing 604/150 with 256MB of RAM, with a 30/1600 ThunderColor graphics card). There she opened the image and made adjustments to the color channels using the Curves tool. Curves is the tool Olson uses most frequently to correct color balance and density. This all-purpose tool allows her to make small, incremental adjustments in the highlights, midtones and shadows.

By reading her on-screen densitometer, Olson first identified her highlights and adjusted them to 9 percent. She then located her black point, the darkest area on the image, and adjusted that to approximately 92 percent. From experience, she knew that the Iris output device this image was intended for would hold detail on watercolor paper at these settings. Now it was time to bring drama back to the image. By "pushing and pulling" the curve that remained between her highlight and shadow points, she recreated the feel of the original fiber-base print.

Nancy and John Olson • NancyScans, Inc. • 273 Highland Rd. • Chatham, NY 12037 • Phone: (800) 604-1199 • Fax: (800) 551-9116

> "WHILE TODAY'S HARDWARE OFFERS PUSH-BUTTON SCANNING, THE KNOWLEDGE OF COLOR THEORY, DARKROOM TECHNIQUES, PRINTING AND PREPRESS ARE STILL AT THE HEART OF A GREAT CUSTOM SCAN. TRUE CRAFTSMANSHIP CONTINUES TO BE THE BLEND OF ART AND TECHNOLOGY."

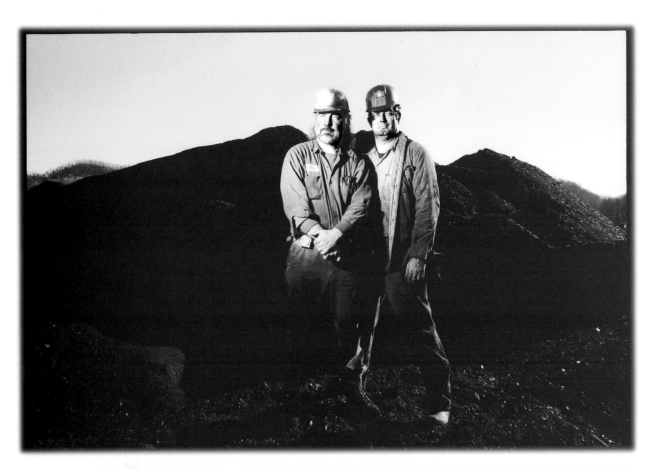

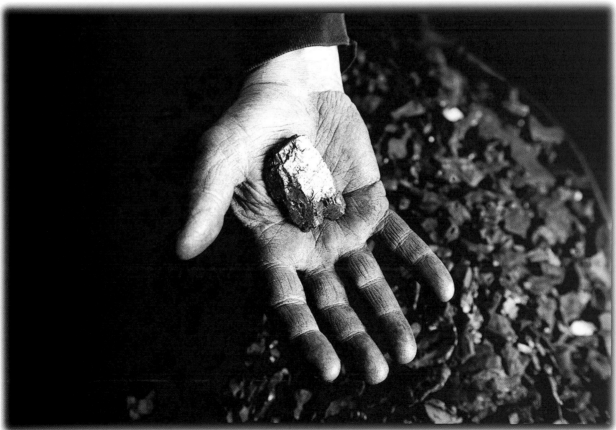

BOB AND LOIS SCHLOWSKY

Schlowsky Computer Imagery

Schlowsky Computer Imagery is located in the bucolic woods west of Boston. The husband-and-wife team's combined backgrounds in traditional photography and illustration give them a knack for combining true artistry with the latest digital tools in the production of jobs for such internationally known clients as Pfizer, Titlest and Hewlett-Packard.

Most of the Schlowskys' work is digitally based; however, Bob Schlowsky continues to use his 35mm cameras to acquire material for the couple's library of imagery. Recently, the Schlowskys were spotted in the Kakakdu region of Australia capturing future digital fodder. Stock slides are the backbone of the team's dreamlike digital photo illustrations.

"CALIBRATING YOUR SYSTEM IS THE MOST IMPORTANT AND ONE OF THE MOST PAINSTAKING THINGS YOU MUST DO IF YOU WANT TO BE SERIOUS ABOUT DIGITAL IMAGERY."

Much of their income these days is derived from reselling their "stock" digital compositions. They produce forty to fifty per year, typically mastering the images to CDR (CD Recordable disks) before submitting them. The Schlowskys' work is carried by Tony Stone Images and is sold throughout the world.

A typical stock digital illustration (for example, the image on the following page) may be composed of twelve layers or so, utilizing Adobe Illustrator line art, scanned 2¼" and 35mm chromes from their vast stock photography collection, and digital camera captures. The final "flattened" image results in a file size of 50MB or more—plenty good enough for a typical magazine spread.

The Schlowskys scan their images using their venerable Leafscan 45 transparency scanner. Digital photographs are generated using either Leaf Digital Camera Back or a Leaf CatchLight attached to a Hasselblad body. Before images are assembled into a montage, they are brought into Photoshop, running on a Macintosh 950, where Unsharp Masking is applied. Individual scans are captured at 3,000 x 4,000 samples (for the Leaf-scan 45) and 2,000 x 2,000 samples on the Leaf Digital Back. All images are scanned at a resolution to maintain at least 225 spi when scaled to 100 to 150 percent of their final sizes. Bob supplies images preseparated into CMYK utilizing custom lookup tables that he has developed for all their equipment.

Lois uses HiRes QFX software from Ron Scott Inc. on a PC clone to combine all the images into a final montage. Proofs are made using either 3M Matchprint, IRIS, or Kodak XL7700 (for work-in-progress view). Software, scanner, monitor and proofer are all painstakingly calibrated using Bob's proprietary lookup tables.

Bob and Lois Schlowsky • Schlowsky Computer Imagery • 73 Old Rd. • Weston, MA 02193 • Phone: (781) 899-5110 • Fax: (781) 647-1608 • E-mail: bob@schlowsky.com

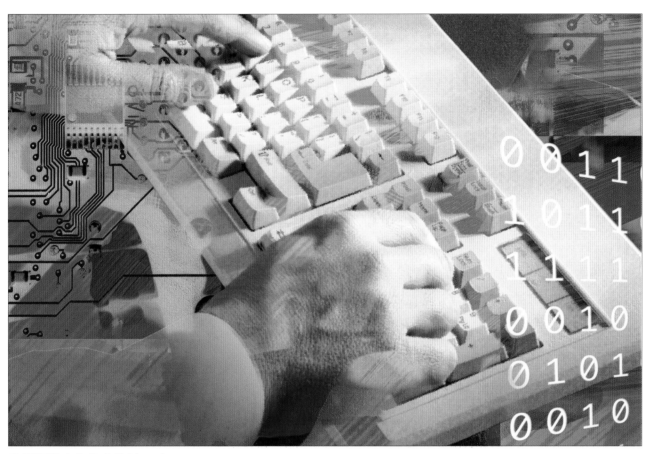

© 1997 Bob & Lois Schlowsky

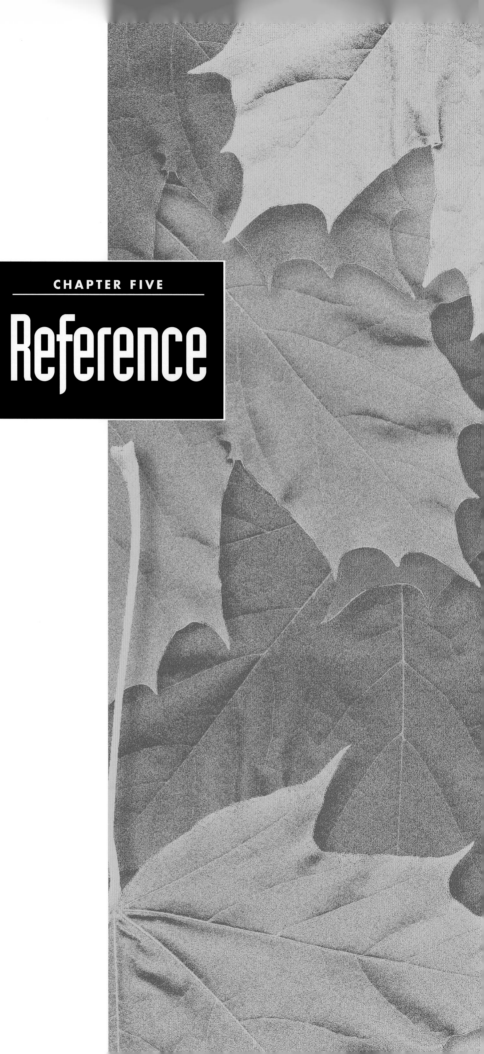

CHAPTER FIVE

Reference

Suggested Reading

ADVANCED ADOBE PHOTOSHOP, Hayden Books, Indianapolis, IN, 1994.

THE COLOR MAC: PRODUCTION TECHNIQUES, SECOND EDITION, by Marc D. Miller and Randy Zaucha, Hayden Books, Indianapolis, IN, 1995.

THE COLOR RESOURCE COMPLETE COLOR GLOSSARY: FROM DESKTOP TO COLOR ELECTRONIC PREPRESS, by Miles Southworth, Graphic Arts Publishing Co., Livonia, 1992.

THE COLOR SCANNER BOOK, by Stephen Beale and James Cavuoto, Micro Publishing, Torrance, CA, 1995.

THE COMPLETE SCANNER HANDBOOK FOR DESKTOP PUBLISHING, by David D. Busch, Business One Irwin, Homewood, IL, 1992.

DESIGNER PHOTOSHOP, SECOND EDITION, by Rob Day, Random House, Inc., New York, 1995.

FOUR COLORS, ONE IMAGE, by Mattias Nyman, Peachpit Press, Berkeley, CA, 1993.

HALFTONE EFFECTS, by Peter Bridgewater and Gerald Woods, Chronicle Books, San Francisco, 1993.

IMAGING ESSENTIALS, by Luanne Seymour Cohen, Russell Brown and Tanya Wendling, Hayden Books, Indianapolis, IN, 1993.

AN INTRODUCTION TO DIGITAL SCANNING, Agfa-Gevaert, Agfa Educational Publishing, Belgium, http://www.agfahome.com.

THE PHOTOSHOP WOW! BOOK, by Linnea Dayton and Jack Davis, Peachpit Press, Berkeley, CA, 1994.

PRODUCTION ESSENTIALS, by Luanne Seyour Cohen, Russell Brown and Tanya Wendling, Hayden Books, Indianapolis, IN, 1994.

REAL WORLD SCANNING AND HALFTONES, by David Blatner and Steve Roth, Peachpit Press, Berkeley, CA, 1993.

START WITH A SCAN: A GUIDE TO TRANSFORMING SCANNED PHOTOS AND OBJECTS INTO HIGH ART, by Janet Ashford and John Odam, Peachpit Press, Berkeley, CA, 1996.

Professional Organizations/Services

AMERICAN INSTITUTE OF GRAPHIC ARTISTS (AIGA), New York, NY 10010; (212) 242-6438; http://www.aiga.com
The oldest professional organization in the United States dedicated to graphic design issues. Local chapters throughout the country put on an assortment of lectures/classes/events.

ASSOCIATION FOR GRAPHICS ARTS TRAINING, Nashville, TN; (615) 386-6124
Training and referrals for the graphic arts.

COLOREXPERT INC., Toronto, Canada; (416) 540-3894; http://www.colorexpert.com [represented by Image Club at (800) 387-9193]
Produces a series of interactive CD-ROM training programs covering all manner of color imaging topics.

THE GRAPHIC ARTS TECHNICAL FOUNDATION (GATF), Pittsburgh, PA; (800) 214-1120, (412) 621-6941
GATF publishes a list of postsecondary printing and graphic arts programs offered at U.S. institutions.

INTERNATIONAL PREPRESS ASSOCIATION, Edina, MN; (612) 896-1908
Training and referrals for prepress.

UNITED DIGITAL ARTISTS, New York, NY; (212) 777-7200; http://www.uda.com
Basic and advanced training in popular desktop publishing applications and processes. Classes take place at the Apple Market Center on the 29th floor of the Citibank building.

Software
Scanning-Specific Software

AGFA DIVISION BAYER CORPORATION, 200 Ballardvale, Wilmington, MA 01887-1069; (800) 685-4271, (800) 879-2632; fax: (508) 658-4193; http://www.agfahome.com

ColorTune—Productive ICC profile creation and editing. Macintosh.

FotoTune—Agfa's color management system includes over 100 ColorTag profiles for various scanners, monitors and printers; an IT8 color reference target; and calibration software. Macintosh and Windows.

FotoLook— Driver software for Agfa scanners.

BINUSCAN, INC., 505 Fifth Ave., Suite 1800, New York, NY 10017; (212) 681-0600; fax: (212) 681-0603; http://www.binuscan.com

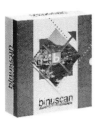

ColorPro Package 3.0—Compatible with scanners, digital cameras and Photo CDs. Automates color or grayscale corrections and CMYK color separations; converts RGB to grayscale. Automatically sets highlights, shadows, contrast balance, saturation, etc. Macintosh and Windows.

BLUERIDGE TECHNOLOGIES, 664 H Zachary Taylor Highway, Flint Hill, VA 22627; (540) 675-3015; fax: (540) 675-3130; http://www.blueridge.com

OPTIX—Industrial-strength document management system that is optimized for Macintosh, Windows and the Internet.

CYTOPIA SOFTWARE, 1735 E. Bayshore Rd., Suite 30B, Redwood City, CA 94063; (415) 948-0396; fax: (415) 364-4592; http://www.cytopia.com

PhotoLab— Set of integrated photographic plug-ins for Photoshop. Includes "Accurate Color Negative Inversal" and others.

ScanPrepPro—Totally automated image processing, scanner automation, descreening plug-in for Photoshop.

ENVISIONS SOLUTIONS TECHNOLOGY, INC., 3485 Kifer Rd., Santa Clara, CA 95051; (800) 365-7226; fax: (408) 735-0222; http://www.envisions.com

DynaScan 3.0—Produces sharp, balanced scans automatically; 32-bit code; zoomable preview windows; more precise color controls; automatic image recognition. Macintosh and Windows.

EXTENSIS CORPORATION, 55 SW Yamhill St., Fourth Floor, Portland, OR 97204; (503) 274-2020; fax: (503) 274-0530; http://www.extensis.com

Intellihance—An intelligent tool that optimizes your photo images in a single step and is compatible with other applications that use Photoshop plug-ins. Macintosh and Windows.

FLAMINGO BAY/IMAGEXPRESS, 1121 Casa Nova Court, Lawrenceville, GA 30244; (770) 564-9924; fax: (770) 564-1632; http://www.scanprep.com

ScanPrepPro — Totally automated image processing, scanner automation, descreening plug-in for Photoshop. Supports a wide range of scanners. Macintosh.

JETSOFT DEVELOPMENT COMPANY, 629 Old State Route 74, Suite #1, Cincinnati, OH 45244; (800) 374-7401; fax: (513) 528-8670; http://www.jetsoft-dev.com

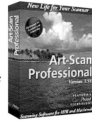

Art-Scan Professional—Powerful, easy-to-use third-party scanning software for a wide variety of desktop scanners. A great way to breathe life into your old scanner. Macintosh and Windows.

LINOTYPE-HELL (HEIDELBERG USA), Hauppauge, NY; (800) 842-9721; http://www.linotype.com

Linocolor—Complete, high-end color management solution for both Macintosh and Windows.

MONACO SYSTEMS, INC., 100 Burtt Rd., Suite 110, Andover, MA 01810; (508) 749-9944; fax: (508) 749-9977

MonacoCOLOR—Color correction, color separation software; Photoshop plug-in; IT8 targets for accurate scanner calibration; selective color correction; automatic image enhancement.

MonacoMATCH—Scan-to-print calibration; includes XRite DTP 51; ICC (ColorSync) compatible.

MonacoEXPERT—Selective color correction; Photoshop plug-in.

SECOND GLANCE SOFTWARE, 7248 Sunset Ave. NE, Bremerton, WA 98311; (306) 692-3694; fax: (800) 682-3041, (360) 692-9241; http://www.secondglance.com

ScanTastic ps (for the Macintosh)—ScanTastic ps provides direct scanner access from within Photoshop. Available versions include support for selected scanners from Apple, Epson and Hewlett-Packard. ScanTastic ps features a unique icon bar that provides a simple method for users to choose a resolution based on output requirements. Other functions include a "live," zoomable, resizable preview that automatically rescans; automatic image balance; tone curves; sharpening; saturation correction; and variable depth support.

SOUTHWEST SOFTWARE, INC., 3435 Greystone Dr., Suite 104, Austin, TX 78731; (512) 345-2493; fax: (512) 345-2697

ProofCheck—Provides quality certification for all proofs, remote or local, digital or traditional. Ensures that your proof accurately predicts press conditions and rejects any proof that does not meet your quality standards.

Color Encore—A feature-rich calibration suite for the color professional. Modules for monitors, scanners, press correction, copiers and imagesetters. Fully integrated with the prepress environment.

RIP Master II—Production control software for imagesetters gives you production condition and calibration monitoring tools as well as job logs, configurable job slugs and a status window.

STALKER SOFTWARE, 655 Redwood Hwy., Mill Valley, CA 94941; (800) 262-4722; fax: (415) 383-7461; http://www.stalker.com

SCSIShare — A control panel that enables sharing a scanner over an Appletalk./Ethernet network from within Photoshop. Macintosh.

ScanShare — A chooser-level device driver that enables sharing an Apple brand scanner over an Appletalk./Ethernet network from within Photoshop. Macintosh.

Other Related Software

ADOBE SYSTEMS INC., 345 Park Ave., San Jose, CA 95110; (415) 961-4400, (800) 833-6687; http://www.adobe.com

Adobe Photoshop—The de facto-standard image manipulation software. Macintosh and Windows.

Adobe Streamline—A robust, stand-alone autotracing tool. Macintosh and Windows.

Adobe Photo Deluxe—Entry-level image manipulation software based on Adobe's Photoshop engine. Macintosh and Windows.

APPLE COMPUTER INC., 1 Infinite Loop, Cupertino, CA 95014; (800) 776-2333, (408) 996-1010; fax: (408) 974-8932; http://www.apple.com

QuickTime—Core system image, video and sound technology. Macintosh and Windows.

ColorSync—Core system color management technology using CIELAB color engine and ICC profiles. Macintosh.

CAERE CORPORATION, 100 Cooper Court, Los Gatos, CA 95030; (800) 535-7226, (408) 395-7000; fax: (408) 354-2743; http://www.caere.com

OmniPage Pro 6.0—Optical character recognition (OCR) software that converts documents into editable text, eliminating the need to retype information. Macintosh and Windows.

CANDELA LTD., 1676 E. Cliff Rd., Burnsville, MN 55377-1300; (612) 894-8890; fax: (612) 894-8840; http://www.candelacolor.com

ColorSynergy 2.0—The least expensive complete package for ColorSync profile creation. Macintosh.

CANTO SOFTWARE, 330 Townsend St., Suite 212, San Francisco, CA 94107; (415) 905-0300; fax: (415) 905-0315; http://www.canto-software.com

Cumulus Media Management—Scriptable image editing, color correction, color management and scanning support for many popular desktop scanners. Sample scripts, adapters and support of ColorSync 2.0 included. Macintosh.

THE COLOR PARTNERSHIP, 2002 Jimmy Durante Blvd., Suite 315, Delmar, CA 92014; (800) 554-8688, (619) 259-8688; fax: (619) 259-8709; http://www.colorpar.com

Profile/80—The first spectral color management system. Generates custom ICC printer profiles. ColorSync compatible, using only eighty color patches to create profile. Macintosh.

SoftProof—A Photoshop plug-in allowing users to color-correct images in a soft proofing mode utilizing ColorSync profiles. Macintosh.

OptiCal—Cross-platform monitor calibration system for both Macintosh and Silicon Graphics workstations. Calibrates monitors to preset industry standards, various gamma response curves and user-definable color settings.

ColorBatch—A stand-alone application that batch-processes images through ColorSync source and destination profiles. Macintosh.

DAYSTAR DIGITAL, 5556 Atlanta Highway, Flowery Branch, GA 30542; (800) 962-2077; http://www.daystar.com

ColorMatch—Color management system that includes monitor calibration, Kodak device profiles, color correction, CMYK preview, and support for Photoshop, QuarkXPress and PageMaker. Optional 8-bit color colorimeter. Macintosh.

EASTMAN KODAK COMPANY, 901 Elmgrove Rd., Rochester, NY 14653; fax: (716) 726-9460; http://www.kodak.com

Kodak Photo CD Access Plus—Stand-alone Photo CD image capture application. Macintosh and Windows.

FRACTAL DESIGN CORPORATION, P.O. Box 66959, Scotts Valley, CA 95067; (800) 846-1111, (408) 430-4000; fax: (408) 438-9671; http://www.fractal.com (*see also* http://www.metatools.com)

Fractal Design Painter—Natural-media paint and image-editing program for Macintosh and Windows.

Fractal Design Poser—The remarkable 3-D human-figure creation reference tool. Macintosh and Windows.

JAG II, JAG for Windows—Jaggies Are Gone! Patented anti-aliasing technique eliminates the "jaggies" in bitmapped images and animations through resolution boosting and anti-aliasing. Macintosh and Windows.

Ray Dream Studio—Cutting-edge 3-D illustration and animation for Windows 95, Windows NT, Windows 3.1. Macintosh and Power Macintosh.

KOFAX IMAGE PRODUCTS, 3 Jenner St., Irvine, CA 92718; (714) 727-1733; fax: (714) 727-3144

Kofax Ascent Capture—For high-volume scanning and indexing.

NetScan—Workgroup scanner-sharing solution for Hewlett-Packard ScanJet scanners.

METATOOLS, INC., 6303 Carpinteria Ave., Carpinteria, CA 93013; (805) 566-6220; fax: (805) 566-6385; http://www.metatools.com (*see also* http://www.fractal.com)

Kai's Power Tools—Incredible plug-in special effects (gradients, textures, fractals, spheres, animation) for Photoshop and other plug-in compatible products. Macintosh, Power Macintosh, Windows 3.1 and Windows 95.

Convolver—Creative and corrective custom filter generator for Photoshop and other plug-in compatible products. Macintosh, Power Macintosh, Windows 3.1, Windows NT and Windows 95.

Bryce 2—Stand-alone 3-D landscape generator. Macintosh, Power Macintosh, Windows 95 and Windows NT.

RON SCOTT, INC., 1000 Jackson Blvd., Houston, TX 77006; (713) 529-5868; fax: (713) 529-9370; http://www.qfx.com

QFX for Windows 95 and Windows NT—The ultimate image-editing software for Intel, DEC Alpha and NEC MIPS graphics systems. Now includes color separations.

XEROX CORPORATION, 9 Centennial Dr., Peabody, MA 01960; (800) 248-6550, x3, (508) 977-2000, (508) 977-2435; http://www.xerox.com

TextBridge Pro 98—Easy-to-use OCR software for any TWAIN or ISIS scanner. Macintosh and Windows.

Pagis Pro 97—Full-featured scanning software completely integrated in Win 95/NT desktop. http://www.pagis.com

Digital Cameras

APPLE COMPUTER INC., 1 Infinite Loop, Cupertino, CA 95014; (800) 538-9696, (408) 996-1010; fax: (408) 974-8932; http://www.apple.com

QuickTake 200—Lightweight, portable digital color camera. 24-bit color, 640 x 480 optical resolution, LCD viewer. ColorSync compatible. Stores twenty high-res images. Includes Adobe PhotoDeluxe and Adobe PageMill. Optional 4MB card stores forty high-res images. Macintosh.

CHINON AMERICA, INC., 600 Corporate Court, Building C, Middlesex Business Center, South Plainfield, NJ 07080; (800) 932-0374; fax: (908) 757-2971

ES-3000—24-bit color, three selectable resolution modes, 640 x 480 optical resolution. Macintosh and Windows.

DICOMED, Minneapolis, MN; (800) 888-7979, (888) DICOMED; fax: (612) 895-3258; http://www. dicomed.com

Bigshot—Pro-level, 6cm square, 4,096 x 4,096 sample, digital camera back for Hassleblad cameras. Macintosh.

Field Pro—Pro-level, 4" x 5", 6,000 x 7,520 sample, digital camera back for all 4 x 5 cameras. Includes portable hard disk. Macintosh Powerbook.

EASTMAN KODAK COMPANY, Diams 2/5, State 901 Elmgrove Rd., Rochester, NY 14653; (800) 242-2424, (716) 726-9488; fax: (716) 726-9460; http://www. kodak.com

Kodak Professional DCS 460—36-bit color, 2,036 x 3,060 optical resolution. Uses Nikon body with

PCMCIA card. Macintosh and Windows.

Kodak Professional DCS 420—36-bit color, 1,012 x 1,524 optical resolution. Uses Nikon body with PCMCIA card. Macintosh and Windows.

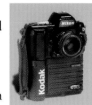

Kodak Digital Science DC40—24-bit color, 768 x 504 optical resolution, PictureWorks PhotoEnhancer. Macintosh and Windows.

EPSON AMERICA, INC., 20770 Madrona Ave., P.O. Box 2903, Torrance, CA 90509; (800) 922-8911, (310) 782-0770; fax: (310) 782-5220; http://www.epson.com

PhotoPC 500—24-bit color, two selectable resolution modes, 640 x 480 optical resolution. Autofocus. Stores up to thirty high-res images. Accepts 37mm videocamcorder lenses and filters. Macintosh and Windows.

LEAF SYSTEMS INC., 8 Oak Park Dr., Bedford, MA 01730; (617) 275-5150; fax: (617) 280-7120; http:// www.scitex.com

Lumina—Unique, midlevel, scanner/camera. 30-bit color, lens mounted, 3,600-line resolution. Macintosh and Windows.

Leaf Digital Back—High-end digital back for Hasselblad and Mamiya studio cameras. 24-bit color, 2,000 x 2,000 pixel. Macintosh.

POLAROID, 565 Technology Square, Cambridge, MA 02139; (617) 386-2000; fax: (617) 386-3584; http://www.polaroid.com

PDC-2000—Midlevel, autofocus digital camera. 800 x 1,200 pixel (interpolated to 1,600 x 1,200). Macintosh and Windows.

Flatbed Scanners

AGFA DIVISION BAYER CORPORATION, 200 Ballardvale St., Wilmington, MA 01887-1069; (800) 685-4271, (508) 658-5600; fax: (508) 658-4193; http://www. agfahome.com

SnapScan—Entry-level, 5.5" x 11.7" (14.0cm x 29.7cm) scan area, 24-bit RGB, 300 x 600 spi. Optional transparency adapter and automatic document feeder. Macintosh and Windows.

StudioScan II Si—Entry-level, 8.5" x 14" (21.6cm x 35.6cm), 400 x 800 spi. Optional transparency adapter. Macintosh and Windows.

StudioStar—Entry-level, 8.5" x 14" (21.6cm x 35.6cm), 30-bit RGB, 600 x 1,200 spi. Optional transparency adapter and automatic document feeder. Macintosh and Windows.

Arcus II—Midlevel flatbed scanner. 8.2" x 14" (21.6cm x 27.9cm), one-pass, 36-bit color, 600 x 1,200 spi. Scans both reflective and transmissive. Batch scanning. Dynamic range of 3.0 Dmax. Macintosh, Windows and UNIX.

DuoScan—Midlevel, 8" x 14" (20.3cm x 35.6cm),

36-bit color, 1,000 x 2,000 spi. Scans both reflective and transmissive. Dynamic range of 3.3 Dmax. Batch scanning. Macintosh, Windows and UNIX.

APPLE COMPUTER INC., 1 Infinite Loop, Cupertino, CA 95014; (800) 776-2333, (408) 996-1010; fax: (408) 974-8932; http://www.apple.com

Apple Color OneScanner 1200/30—Entry-level flatbed scanner. 8.5" x 14" (21.6cm x 35.6cm), 30 bit, 600 x 1,200 spi. ColorSync compatible. Optional automatic document feeder. Optional transparency adapter. Macintosh and Windows.

Apple Color OneScanner 600/27—Entry-level flatbed scanner. 8.5" x 14" (21.6cm x 35.6cm), 27-bit color, 300 x 600 spi. ColorSync compatible. Optional automatic document feeder. Macintosh and Windows.

CANON COMPUTER SYSTEMS, INC., 2995 Redhill Ave., Costa Mesa, CA 92626-5048; (800) 848-4123, (714) 438-3000; fax: (714) 438-3795; http://www.canon.com

IX-4015—Entry-level flatbed scanner. 8.5" x 11" (21.6cm x 27.9cm), 24-bit color, 400 x 800 spi. Optional automatic document feeder. Macintosh and Windows.

IX-4025—Entry-level, 8.5" x 11" (21.6cm x 27.9cm), 24-bit color, 300 x 600 spi. Optional automatic document feeder. Macintosh and Windows.

DPI ELECTRONIC IMAGING SYSTEMS, 629 Old State Route 74, Suite 1, Cincinnati, OH 45244; (800) 597-3837, (513) 528-8668; fax: (513) 528-8668; http://www.dpi-scanner-authority.com

ArtGetter—Midlevel flatbed scanner. 8.5" x 11" (21.6cm x 27.9cm), 30-bit color, 600 x 1,200 spi. OEM version of the UMAX Vista S12. Macintosh and Windows.

EPSON AMERICA, INC., 20770 Madrona Ave., P.O. Box 2903, Torrance, CA 90509; (800) 922-8911, (310) 782-0770; fax: (310) 782-5220; http://www.epson.com

ES-1000C—Entry-level (optical) flatbed scanner. 8.5" x 11" (21.6cm x 27.9cm), 30-bit color, 400 x 800 spi. Bidirectional parallel and SCSI ports. Includes imaging-editing and OCR software. Optional transparency and sheet feed adapters. Macintosh and Windows.

Expression 636—Midlevel (optical) flatbed scanner. 8.5" x 11" (21.6cm x 27.9cm), 36-bit color, 600 x 600 spi. Dmax=3.0. Bidirectional parallel and SCSI ports. Includes image-editing and OCR software. Optional transparency unit and sheet feeder. Macintosh and Windows.

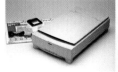

FUJITSU COMPUTER PRODUCTS OF AMERICA, INC., 2904 Orchard Parkway, San Jose, CA 95134-2009; (800) 626-4686; fax: (408) 894-1706; http://www.fujitsu.com

ScanPartner 10C—Entry-level flatbed scanner. 8.5" x 14" (21.6cm x 35.6cm), 24-bit color, 300 x 600 spi. Optional automatic document feeder. Macintosh and Windows.

HEWLETT-PACKARD COMPANY, P.O. Box 58059, MS5111L-SJ, Santa Clara, CA 95051-8059; (800) 722-6538; http://www.hp.com/go/scanjet

ScanJet 5p - Entry-level flatbed scanner. 8.5" x 11.7" (21.6 cm x 29.7 cm), 24 bit, 300-spi optical. Includes image-editing and OCR software. SCSI cable and SCSI adapter for the PC. Macintosh and Windows.

ScanJet 6100Cse - Mid-level flatbed scanner. 8.5" x 14" (21.6 cm x 35.6 cm), 30 bit, 600-spi optical. Includes image-editing and OCR software. SCSI cable and SCSI adapter for the PC. Includes 35mm slide adapter. Optional transparency or automatic document feeder. Macintosh and Windows.

KYE INTERNATIONAL CORP., 2605 E. Cedar St., Ontario, CA 91761-8511; (800) 456-7593, (909) 923-3510; fax: (909) 923-1469; http://www.genius-kye.com

Genius ColorPage-SP2—Entry-level color flatbed scanner. 8.5" x 13.5" (21.6cm x 34.3cm), 24-bit color, 300 x 600 spi. Includes image-editing and OCR software. Optional transparency adapter and auto document feeder. Macintosh and Windows.

LACIE LIMITED, 8700 SW Creekside Place, Beaverton, OR 97008; (800) 999-0143, (503) 520-9100; http://www.lacie.com

Silverscanner II—Entry-level flatbed scanner. 8.5" x 11" (21.6cm x 35.6cm), 24-bit color, 400 x 800 spi. Optional transparency adapter. Macintosh and Windows.

LINOTYPE-HELL (HEIDELBERG), Hauppauge, NY; (800) 842-9721; http://www.linotype.com

Saphir—High-end flatbed scanner. 36-bit color, 8.4" x 11.7" (21.3cm x 29.7cm), 600 x 1,200 spi. Dmax=3.2. Includes LinoColor VisualLab software. Macintosh and Windows.

Saphir Ultra—High-end flatbed scanner. 36-bit color, 8.4" x 11.7" (21.3cm x 29.7cm), 1,000 x 2,000 spi. Dmax=3.3. Includes LinoColor VisualLab software. Macintosh and Windows.

Opal—Midlevel flatbed scanner. 30-bit color, 12" x 17" (30.5cm x 43.2cm) image area, 400 x 800 spi or 800 x 1,600 (zoomable) spi. Dmax=3.0. Includes LinoColor VisualLab software. Macintosh and Windows.

MICROTEK LAB, INC., 3715 Doolittle Dr., Redondo Beach, CA 90278; (800) 654-4160, (310) 297-5000; fax: (310) 297-5050; http://www.mteklab.com

ScanMaker III—Midlevel, 36-bit color, 600 x 1,200 spi, 8.5" x 13.5" (21.6cm x 34.3cm). Dmax=3.4. Transparency adapter included. Automatic document feeder optional. Includes image-editing and OCR software and Microtek DCR color calibration system. Macintosh and Windows.

ScanMaker E6—Entry-level, 30-bit color, 600 x 1,200 spi, 8.5" x 13" (21.6cm x 33cm). Dmax= 3.0. Optional transparency adapter and automatic document feeder. Includes image-editing and OCR software and Microtek DCR color calibration system. Macintosh and Windows.

ScanMaker E3—Entry-level flatbed scanner. 24-bit color, 300 x 600 spi, 8.5" x 13.5" (21.6cm x 34.3cm).

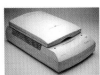 Optional transparent media adapter and automatic document feeder. Includes image-editing and OCR software and Microtek DCR color calibration system. Macintosh and Windows.

MIRROR, 5198 W. Seventy-sixth St., Edine, MN 55439; (800) 654-5294, (612) 832-5406; http://www.mirror.com

Mirror 800 Plus—Entry-level flatbed scanner. 8.5 " x 14" (21.6cm x 35.6cm), 24-bit color, 400 x 800 spi. Optional transparency adapter. Includes image-editing software. Macintosh and Windows.

MUSTEK,1702 McGaw Ave., Irvine, CA 92614; (714) 250-8855; fax: (714) 250-3372; http://www.mustek.com

Paragon 1200—Entry-level flatbed scanner. 8.5" x 14" (21.6cm x 35.6cm), 30-bit color, 600 x 1,200 spi. Macintosh and Windows.

Paragon 800—Entry-level flatbed scanner. 8.5" x 14" (21.6cm x 35.6cm), 30-bit color, 400 x 800 spi. Macintosh and Windows.

Paragon 600—Entry-level flatbed scanner. 8.5"x 11.6" (21.6cm x 29.5cm), 24-bit color, 300 x 600 spi. Macintosh and Windows.

NIKON ELECTRONIC IMAGING, 1300 Walt Whitman Rd., Melville, NY 11747; (800) 526-4566, (516) 547-4355; fax: (516) 547-0305; http://www.nikonusa.com

AX 1200 ScanTouch—Entry-level flatbed scanner. 30-bit color, 600 x 1,200 spi, 8.3" x 14" (21.0cm x 35.6cm). Macintosh and Windows.

PANASONIC, 1 Panasonic Way, Secaucus, NJ 07094; (708) 468-4308, (800) 742-8086; http://www.panasonic.com

FX-RS308Ci—Entry-level flatbed scanner. 600 x 600 spi, 8.5" x 14" (21.6cm x 35.6cm), 24-bit color. Includes Adobe Photoshop LE for Windows.

RELISYS, 919 Hanson Court, Milpitas, CA 95035; (800) 945-0900; http://www.relisys.com

RELI 9624—8.3" x 11.7" (21.0cm x 29.7cm), 24 bit, 600 x 1,200 spi, flatbed scanner with built-in transparency adapter. Optional automatic document feeder. Macintosh and Windows.

RELI 4816—8.5" x 14" (21.6cm x 35.6cm), 24 bit, 400 x 800 spi, flatbed scanner with built-in transparency adapter. Optional automatic document feeder. Macintosh and Windows.

RELI 2412—8.5" x 14" (21.6cm x 35.6cm), 24 bit, 300 x 600 spi, flatbed scanner with built-in transparency adapter. Optional automatic document feeder. Macintosh and Windows.

RICOH CORPORATION PERIPHERAL PRODUCTS DIVISION, 3001 Orchard Parkway, San Jose, CA 95134-2088; (800) 955-3453, (408) 432-8800; fax: (408) 432-9266; http://www.ricoh.com

FS2—Entry-level flatbed scanner. 8.3" x 14" (21.0cm x 35.6cm), 30-bit color, 600 x 1,200 spi. Optional transparency adapter. Macintosh and Windows.

CS-300—Entry-level desktop flatbed scanner. 11" x 17" (27.9cm x 43.2cm), 24-bit color, 300 x 600 spi. Macintosh and Windows.

SHARP ELECTRONICS CORPORATION, SHARP PLAZA, P.O. Box F1, Mahwah, NJ 07430-2135; (800) 237-4277, x3; fax: (201) 529-9637; http://www.sharp=usa.com

JX 610—High-level flatbed scanner. 11" x 17" (27.9cm x 43.2cm), three lamps, 36-bit color, 600 x 600 spi. Optional transparency adapter. Macintosh and Windows

SPARK INTERNATIONAL, INC., P.O. Box 314, Glenview, IL 60025; (708) 998-6640

Spectrum Scan III—Entry-level flatbed scanner with integrated transparency adapter. 8.5" x 11" (21.6cm x 27.9cm), 24-bit color, 600 x 1,200 spi. Optional automatic document feeder. Macintosh and Windows.

Spectrum Scan III+—Entry-level flatbed scanner with integrated transparency adapter. 8.5" x 11" (21.6cm x 27.9cm), 30-bit color, 600 x 1,200 spi. Optional automatic document feeder. Macintosh and Windows.

UMAX TECHNOLOGIES, INC., 3353 Gateway Blvd., Fremont, CA 94538; (800) 562-0311, (510) 651-8883; fax: (510) 651-8834; http://www.umax.com

Astra 610 — Entry-level flatbed. 30-bit color, 300 x 600 spi, 8.5" x 11" (21.6cm x 27.9cm). Available in SCSI or Parallel versions. Macintosh and Windows.

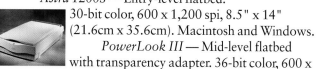

Astra 1200S — Entry-level flatbed. 30-bit color, 600 x 1,200 spi, 8.5" x 14" (21.6cm x 35.6cm). Macintosh and Windows.

PowerLook III — Mid-level flatbed with transparency adapter. 36-bit color, 600 x 1,200 spi, 8.3" x 11.7" (21.0cm x 29.7cm). Macintosh and Windows.

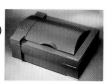

Mirage II — Mid-level flatbed. 36-bit color, 700 x 1,400 spi, 1,400 x 2,800 spi dual lens, 12" x 17" (30.5cm x 43.2cm). Macintosh and Windows.

High-End Scanners

AGFA DIVISION BAYER CORPORATION, 200 Ballardvale St., Wilmington, MA 01887-1069; (800) 685-4271, (508) 658-5600; fax: (508) 658-4193; http://www.agfahome.com

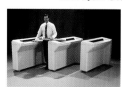

Horizon Ultra—High-end flatbed scanner. 11.7" x 16.5" (29.7cm x 41.9cm), three-pass, 36-bit color, 1,200 x 2,000 spi. Scans both reflective and transmissive. Dynamic range of 3.2D with 3.4Dmax. Features batch scanning. Macintosh, Windows and UNIX.

SelectScan Plus—High-end 8" x 10" (20.3cm x 25.4cm) transmissive, 8" x 11" (20.3cm x 27.9cm) reflective, single pass. Captures data at 16 bits per color, outputs 39-bit RGB, 4,000 x 8,000 spi. Dynamic range of 3.7D with 4.0Dmax. Scans both reflective and tranmissive. Features batch scanning. Macintosh.

ANA TECH/INTERGRAPH, 10499 Bradford Rd., Littleton, CO 80127; (303) 973-6722; fax: (303) 973-7092; http://www.anatech.scanners.com/a_web/

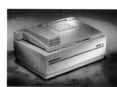

Eagle SLI 3840—Monochrome scanner provides 400-dpi real resolution in a high-speed desktop model. It features a scan width of 38" (96.5cm) and 1 to 800 dpi variable scan resolution, plus 256 levels of grayscale data. The scanner uses a new technology image sensor that allows face-up scanning of documents. The Eagle SLI 3840 scans an E/A0 size document at 200 dpi in only fifteen seconds flat.

Eagle 3640C—Color scanner, priced for affordability in both workstation and high-end PC markets; concurrently scans, classifies, compresses and saves to disk original color documents up to 41" (104.1cm) wide; maximum scan width 36" (91.4cm), with a real scan resolution of 400 dpi.

Eagle 3640—Monochrome scanner, offering true 400-dpi and interpolated 800-dpi resolutions, is designed for document management applications in manufacturing, design engineering, A/E/C and government markets, among others. It additionally

offers 8-bit grayscale, 256 levels of grayscale data and advanced CCD data capture.

Eagle 4080C—Color scanner, priced at less than half the cost of drum-type scanners; concurrently scans, classifies, compresses and saves to disk original color documents up to 41" (104.1cm) wide; maximum scan width 40" (101.6cm), with a real scan resolution of 800 dpi.

Eagle 4080ET—Monochrome scanner offers a real scan resolution of 800 dpi and an interpolated resolution up to 1,600 dpi to users in the GIS/mapping markets. It additionally offers 8-bit grayscale, 256 levels of grayscale data and advanced CCD data capture.

HOWTEK, INC., 21 Park Ave., Hudson, NH 03051; (603) 882-5200; fax: (603) 880-3843; http://www.howtek.com

Scanmaster 7500 Pro—High-end, high-resolution, large-format, production-oriented, multiplatform drum scanner.

Scanmaster 4500—Trade shop color quality; precise reproductions; easy-to-use multiplatform drum scanner.

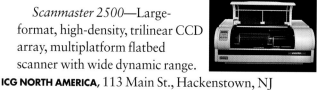

Scanmaster 2500—Large-format, high-density, trilinear CCD array, multiplatform flatbed scanner with wide dynamic range.

ICG NORTH AMERICA, 113 Main St., Hackenstown, NJ 07840; (908) 813-3101; fax: (908) 813-1676; http://www.icg.ltd.uk/showroom.html

308i Callisto—308i desktop scanner. 10.5" x 12.5" (26.7cm x 31.8cm) format, 32-bit color, 4,000 spi. Macintosh.

330i—Deskslide vertical scanner. 9.5" x 18.5" (24.1cm x 47cm).

Camino—Slimline vertical scanner. 12.7" x 18.7" (32.3cm x 47.5cm), 36-bit color, 4,000 spi. Macintosh.

350i—Vertical scanner. 12.5" x 18.7" (31.8cm x 47.5cm), 36-bit color, 4,000 spi. Macintosh.

355i—Vertical scanner. 12.5" x 18.7" (31.8cm x

47.5cm), 36-bit color, 8,000 spi. Macintosh.

Each ICG input product operates through ICG ScanXact color software. ScanXact provides high-end control functionality, two-second artificial intelligence copy setup and mixed media batch scanning. The same

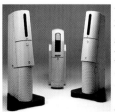

interface is used on all products, making movement from one device to another possible with minimal training. ICG vertical scanners feature QuickMount copy loading, which brings flatbed ease of use to high-quality drum scanning.

IMACON APS., 26 Hejrevej, SK-2400 Copenhagen NV, Denmark; +45 38 88 40 50; fax: +45 38 88 40 52; http://www.imacon.dk

FlexTight—High-end desktop scanner for professional PostScript environments. 42-bit color, 4,800 spi. Transparencies up to 4" x 5"; reflect art up to 32cm x 22cm. Macintosh and Windows.

IMAPRO CORPORATION, 2400 St. Laurent Blvd., Ottawa,

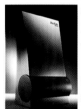

Ontario, Canada K1G 5A4; (613) 738-3000; fax: (613) 738-5038; http://www.imapro.com

QCS-3200—High-end desktop CCD flatbed with transparency adapter. 35-bit color, 3,200 x 1,500 spi, 11" x 17" (27.9cm x 43.2cm). Imapro Winscan (PC) or

Photoshop plug-in (Macintosh).

LINOTYPE-HELL (HEIDELBERG), Hauppauge, NY; (800) 842-9721; http://www.linotype.com

Tango—High-end vertical drum scanner with 11,000-spi data capture and Dmax=4.0. 36-bit color, 7.7" x 18.8" (19.6cm x 47.8cm) image area. Macintosh.

Topaz—High-end flatbed scanner. 36-bit color, 12" x 18" (30.5cm x 45.7cm) image area. Dmax=3.7. Macintosh.

ChromaGraphS 3400—High-end drum scanner. 36-bit color, 20" x 25.6" (50.8cm x 65cm) image area. Includes Cumulus image database. Macintosh.

OPTRONICS INTERNATIONAL, 21 Alpha Road, Chelmsford, MA 01824; (800) 331-7568, (508) 256-4511; fax: (508) 256-1872; http://www.ingr.com/optronics

Optronics ColorGetter Eagle — Incomparable but low-cost, 8,128-dpi, 11" x 15" (27.9cm x 38.1cm) reflective/transmissive PMT drum scanner. Uses ColorRight software. Supports Macintosh and Windows.

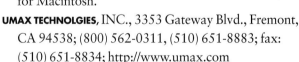

SCANVIEW, INC., 330A Hatch Dr., Foster City, CA 94404; (415) 378-6360; fax: (415) 378-6368; http://www.scanview.com

ScanMate Plus II—Desktop drum scanner. 36-bit color, 2,600 spi, 8.5" x 11" (21.6cm x 27.9cm).

Macintosh and Windows.

ScanMate Magic—Desktop drum scanner. 36-bit color, 2,000 spi, 8.5" x 11.5" (21.6cm x 29.2cm). Macintosh and Windows.

ScanMate 3000—Desktop drum scanner. 36-bit color, 3,000 spi, 8.5" x 11.5" (21.6cm x 29.2cm). Macintosh and Windows.

ScanMate 4000—Desktop drum scanner. 36-bit color, 4,000 spi, 8.75" x 12" (22.2cm x 30.5cm). Macintosh and Windows.

ScanMate 5000—Desktop drum scanner. 36-bit color 5,000 spi, 8.75" x 12" (22.2cm x 30.5cm). Macintosh and Windows.

ScanMate 11000—Desktop drum scanner. 42-bit color, 11,000 spi, 8.75" x 12" (22.2cm x 30.5cm). Macintosh and Windows.

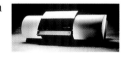

SCITEX, 8 Oak Park Dr., Bedford, MA 01730; (617) 275-5150; fax: (617) 275-3430; http://www.scitex.com

Smart 342 — High end flatbed scanner with built-in transparency capability. 36 bit, large-format 11.8" x 17" (30.0cm x 43.2cm). 1,950 spi (entire platen). Includes Smart Dot application for scanning halftone films. Macintosh.

SCREEN USA, 5110 Tollview Dr., Rolling Meadows, IL 60008; (847) 870-7400; fax: (847) 870-0149; http://www.screenusa.com

Cézanne — Large format 13.4" x 20.8" (34.0cm x 52.8cm), 48 bit, high resolution 5,300-spi flatbed scanner for Macintosh.

SG-8060P — Large format 23.6" x 21.2" (60.0cm x 53.8cm), 48 bit, high resolution 12,000-spi digital drum scanner for Macintosh.

DT-S1045Ai — Large format 12" x 17" (30.5cm x 43.2cm), 48-bit, high-resolution 8,000-spi digital drum scanner for Macintosh.

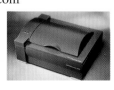

UMAX TECHNOLGIES, INC., 3353 Gateway Blvd., Fremont, CA 94538; (800) 562-0311, (510) 651-8883; fax: (510) 651-8834; http://www.umax.com

PowerLook 3000 — High-end flatbed with moving platen. 42-bit color, 3.6 DMax, 3,048 x 3,048 spi, 1,220 x 3,048 spi dual lens, autofocus, 8" x 11.7" (20.3cm x 29.7cm). Macintosh and Windows.

VISION SHAPE, 1434 West Taft Ave., Orange, CA 92865; (800) 962-3585, (714) 282-2668; fax: (714) 282-2673; http://www.visionshape.com

VS-1251E—Black-and-white page scanner. 200, 240 and 300 spi. GPIB (serial/video, like Fujitsu and Bell & Howell), 5" x 5" (12.7cm x 12.7cm) up to 11"

x 17" (27.9cm x 43.2cm). Windows.

    B-1000—Grayscale check scanner. 100 and 200 spi. Scans forty checks per minute. Windows.

    VS-1000E—2-bit, black-and-white page scanner. 200, 240, 300 and 400 spi. GPIB (serial/video, like Fujitsu and Bell & Howell), 8.5" x 14" (21.6cm x 35.6cm). Windows.

    VS-2500 Duplex—2 bit, black-and-white page scanner. 200, 240 and 300 spi. GPIB (serial/video, like Fujitsu and Bell & Howell), 5" x 5" (12.7cm x 12.7cm) up to 11" x 17" (27.9cm x 43.2cm). Windows.

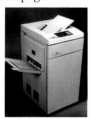

Transparency Scanners

EASTMAN KODAK COMPANY, 901 Elmgrove Rd., Rochester, NY 14653; (800) 242-2424, (716) 726-9488; fax: (716) 726-9460; http://www.kodak.com

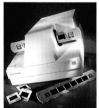

    Kodak Professional RFS 2035 Plus—Midlevel 35mm slide scanner. 2,000-line resolution, 36-bit color. Macintosh and Windows.

    Kodak Professional RFS 3570—Midlevel 35mm slide scanner. 2,000-line resolution, 36-bit color. Macintosh and Windows.

LEAF SYSTEMS INC., 8 Oak Park Dr., Bedford, MA 01730; (617) 275-5150; fax: (617) 280-7120; http://www.scitex.com

    Leafscan 45—High-end multiformat film scanner. 42-bit color, 4,000-line resolution. Macintosh and Windows.

MICROTEK LAB, INC., 3715 Doolittle Dr., Redondo Beach, CA 90278; (800) 654-4160, (310) 297-5000; fax: (310) 297-5050; http://www.mteklab.com

    ScanMaker 35t Plus—Entry-level film scanner. 30-bit color, 1,950 spi, 36 x 36mm maximum scan area. Image-editing software included. Macintosh and Windows.

MINOLTA CORPORATION, 101 Williams Dr., Ramsey, NJ 07446; (201) 825-4000, x5308; fax: (201) 825-0282; http://www.minoltausa.com

    QuickScan 35—Entry-level 35mm film scanner. 30-bit color, 2,820 spi. Macintosh and Windows.

NIKON ELECTRONIC IMAGING, 1300 Walt Whitman Rd., Melville, NY 11747; (800) 526-4566, (516) 547-4355; fax: (516) 547-0305; http://www.nikonusa.com

    Nikon LS 4510 AF—Midlevel slide scanner. 36-bit color, autofocus, 3,600-line resolution, multiformat. Macintosh and Windows.

    Nikon CoolScan II—Entry-level 35mm slide scanner. 24-bit color, 1,850-line resolution. Macintosh and Windows.

    Nikon SuperCoolScan—Midlevel 35mm slide scanner with optional batch operation. 36-bit color, 1,850-line resolution. Macintosh and Windows.

POLAROID, 565 Technology Square, Cambridge, MA 02139; (617) 386-2000; fax: (617) 386-3584; http://www.polaroid.com

    SprintScan 35/LE—Entry-level 35mm film scanner. 30-bit color, 1,950-line resolution. Dmax=3.0. Macintosh and Windows.

    SprintScan 35/ES—Entry-level 35mm film scanner. 30-bit color, 1,350 x 2,700-line resolution. Dmax=3.0. Macintosh and Windows.

    SprintScan 35 Plus—Midlevel 35mm film scanner. 36-bit color, 2,700-line resolution. Dmax=3.4. Macintosh and Windows.

    SprintScan 45—Midlevel multiformat transparency scanner. 36-bit color, 4,000-line resolution. Macintosh and Windows.

Specialty Scanners

A4 TECH (USA) CORP., 20256 Paeso Robles, Walnut, CA 91789; (909) 468-0071; fax: (909) 468-2231

    AG-800—Handheld scanner. Grayscale, 400 spi. Windows.

    PRO-800—Handheld scanner. 24-bit color, 400 spi. Windows.

BELL & HOWELL, 6800 N. McCormick Rd., Chicago, IL 60645; (800) SCAN-494; http://www.bellhowell.com/scanners

    Copiscan 8000 series—Business-use flatbed with autodocument feeder for high-speed, high-volume digital archiving of business documents. Optional duplex capabilities.

CAERE CORPORATION, 100 Cooper Court, Los Gatos, CA 95030; (800) 535-7226, (408) 395-7000; fax: (408) 354-2743; http://www.caere.com

Omniscan—Handheld scanner with 4"- (10.2cm-) wide scanning area. 24-bit color, 400 spi. Macintosh and Windows.

CALCOMP, 2411 West La Palma Ave., P.O. Box 3250, Anaheim, CA 92803-3250; (800) 932-1212, (714) 821-2000; fax: (714) 821-2832; http://www. calcomp.com

ScanPlus III 400T, ScanPlus III 800T, ScanPlus 1200T and *ScanPlus III 1800T*—400, 800, 1,200 and 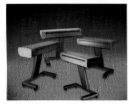 1,800 dpi, respectively; one-pass scanning; low cost; high volume; 256 levels of grayscale; 25 to 1,800 spi; images up to 36" (91.4cm) wide; CadImage/Scan software. Macintosh and Windows.

FUJITSU COMPUTER PRODUCTS OF AMERICA, INC., 2904 Orchard Parkway, San Jose, CA 95134-2009; (800) 626-4686; fax: (408) 894-1706; http://www.fujitsu.com

Scan Partner Jr.—Sheet-fed scanner. 256 grayscale, 300 x 600 spi, 8.5" x 14" (21.6cm x 35.6cm). Macintosh and Windows.

HEWLETT-PACKARD COMPANY, P.O. Box 58059, MS5111L-SJ, Santa Clara, CA 95051-8059; (800) 722-6538; http://www.hp.com/go/scanjet

 ScanJet 5s—Sheet-fed scanner. 8.5" x 30" (21.6cm x 76.2cm), 24-bit color, 300 spi. Includes paper-management software with integrated OCR, AC adapter and parallel cable. Windows.

I.R.I.S. USA, 1600 NW Boca Raton Blvd., Suite 20, Boca Raton, FL 33432; (800) 447-4744, (407) 395-7831; fax: (407) 347-6267; http://www.irisusa.com

IRISPen—Unique pen "line" scanner with built-in OCR in twenty-six languages. Character size from 8 to 22 points. Line length up to 11" (27.9) per scan. 300 spi. Serial/parallel connection. Macintosh and Windows.

LOGITECH, 6505 Kaiser Dr., Fremont, CA 94555; (800) 231-7717, (510) 795-8500; fax: (510) 713-5034; http://www.logitech.com

ScanMan Color—Handheld scanner with 4" (10.2cm) wide scanning area. 24-bit color, 100 to 400 spi. Windows.

PageScan Color—Sheet-fed scanner with flatbed versatility. 24-bit color. Bidirectional parallel port interface. Windows.

MEKEL ENGINEERING, INC., 2800 Saturn St., Brea, CA 92821-6201; (714) 996-5600; fax: (714) 996-5696; http://www.mekel.com

M460XL Microfiche Scanner—Scans all standard formats of 105mm cut microfiche or 16mm jackets. Macintosh.

M500 Microfilm Scanner—Scans 16mm and 35mm microfilm to various storage media. Macintosh.

MICROTEK, 3715 Doolittle Dr., Redondo Beach, CA 90278; (800) 654-4160, (310) 297-5000; fax: (310) 297-5050; http://www.mteklab.com

PageWiz—Single-pass personal scanner. 300 spi; 16 shades of gray, upgradable to 256 shades of gray. Scan, fax, OCR, e-mail, print, annotation, document storage and retrieval functions. Parallel port interface. Windows.

PANASONIC, 1 Panasonic Way, Secaucus, NJ 07094; (708) 468-4308; (800) 742-8086, http://www. panasonic.com

KV-SS50/55—High-performance forty-page/minute scanners; letter size; 200 spi. Duplex scanning capabilities (KV-SS55 SCSI). One hundred-page automatic document feeder; flexible document handling (business card to legal).

POLAROID, 565 Technology Square, Cambridge, MA 02139; (617) 386-2000; fax: (617) 386-3584; http://www.polaroid.com

CS-500 Print-to-Press—Unique 4" x 6" (10.2cm x 15.2cm) hardware/software scanning solution for time-sensitive production environments. Optimized for Polaroid professional films. Macintosh and Windows.

PhotoPad—4" x 6" (10.2cm x 15.2cm) sheet-fed. 24-bit color, 400 spi. Parallel interface. Includes TWAIN support and calibration software. Windows.

UMAX TECHNOLOGIES, INC., 3353 Gateway Blvd., Fremont, CA 94538; (800) 562-0311, (510) 651-8883; fax: (510) 651-8834; http://www.umax.com

BizCard Reader—Small, inexpensive, parallel port-driven, business card scanner for Macintosh and Windows.

Page Office Duo—Sheet-fed. 8-bit grayscale, 300 spi, 8.5" x 14" (21.2cm x 35.6cm). Macintosh and Windows (in one box).

VISIONSHAPE, 1434 W. Taft Ave., Orange, CA 92865; (714) 282-2668; fax: (714) 282-2673; http://www. visionshape.com

VS-1000E—Forty-page/minute simplex scanner. Size 8.5" x 11" to 14" (21.2cm x 27.9cm to 35.6cm),

200 to 400 spi. Straight paper path; built-in automatic document feeder. Video RS232 interface with Dunord, Kofax, Xionics and all Fujitsu compatible boards. Includes a double-feed detector. Windows.

VS-1251E—Forty-page/minute simplex scanner. Size 5" x 5" (12.7cm x 12.7cm) up to 11" x 17" (27.9cm x 43.2cm), 200 to 300 spi. Straight paper path; built-in automatic document feeder. Video RS232 interface with Dunord, Kofax, Xionics and all Fujitsu compatible boards. Includes a double-feed detector. Windows.

VS-2500D—Duplex, thirty-eight pages and seventy-six images per minute scanner. Designed for volume production of thousands of documents per day. Includes scanner, compression cards, scanning software. Windows.

XEROX, 290 Woodcliff Dr., Building 818, Fairport, NY 14450; (716) 383-9321; http://www.xerox.com

DocuImage 620S—High-volume flatbed document scanner for OCR use. Grayscale, 11.6" x 17" (29.5cm x 43.2cm), 400 x 600 spi. Windows.

Other Related Hardware

APS TECHNOLOGIES, 6131 Deramus, Kansas City, MO 64120; (816) 483-1600; http://www.apstech.com

SCSI Sentry—Active termination for SCSI chains eliminates SCSI electrical problems for any SCSI-equipped computer.

LASERGRAPHICS, INC., 20 Ada, Irvine, CA 92718; (800) 727-2655

LFR Mark III—Midlevel slide recorder. 8,000-line resolution. Macintosh and Windows.

LIGHT SOURCE, 4040 Civic Center Dr., Fourth Floor, San Rafael, CA 94903; (415) 466-4200; fax: (415) 492-8011; http://www.ls.com

Colortron II—Affordable, accurate and easy-to-use color spectrophotometer, densitometer and monitor calibrator. Macintosh and Windows.

WACOM TECHNOLOGY CORPORATION, 501 SE Columbia Shores Blvd., Suite 300, Vancouver, WA 98661; (206) 750-8882; http://www.wacom.com

ArtPad II Graphics Tablet—Entry-level graphics tablet in 4" x 5" size.

ArtZ II Graphics Tablets—Professional graphics tablets available in 6" x 8", 12" x 12", 12" x 18" and 18" x 25" for Macintosh, PC, SGI. 6" x 8" also comes in ADB port version for the Macintosh.

Pick the Right SPI

Sample Rate

Most scanning experts advise that good quality halftones require a scan from 1 to 2 pixels per printed halftone dot. However, I have found that a 1-to-1 pixel per halftone dot ratio is adequate for many purposes. I use that sample rate for all my cover designs for the Boston Computer Society IBM User Group Newsletter, *PC Report*. The obvious advantage of a 1-to-1 sample rate is smaller file size. For instance, each of my *PC Report* covers is just 6.3MB. A scan of 2 pixels per halftone dot would result in an image nearly four times as big!

Although purists insist that optimal imagesetting requires a 2-to-1 sample rate, newer thinking suggests that a 1.5-to-1 sampling rate is more than a good compromise.

Optimal spi settings at 1.0 sampling ratio

	HALFTONE SCREEN FREQUENCY				
SPI	**65**	**85**	**100**	**133**	**150**
75	115%	88%	75%	56%	50%
90	138%	106%	90%	68%	60%
100	154%	118%	100%	75%	67%
120	185%	141%	120%	90%	80%
150	231%	176%	150%	113%	100%
180	277%	212%	180%	135%	120%
200	308%	235%	200%	150%	133%
210	323%	247%	210%	158%	140%
240	369%	282%	240%	180%	160%
270	415%	318%	270%	203%	180%
300	462%	353%	300%	226%	200%
360	554%	424%	360%	271%	240%
400	615%	471%	400%	301%	267%
480	738%	565%	480%	361%	320%
600	923%	706%	600%	451%	400%
800	1,231%	941%	800%	602%	533%
1,200	1,846%	1,412%	1,200%	902%	800%

Calculating the optimal scan for a given output is relatively easy. Just plug in the enlargement or reduction percentage you want for the appropriate halftone screen.

My feeling is that images on low-grade, coarse or uncoated papers and background images can get away with 1-to-1 sampling while images on high-quality coated stock or images that may need to be resized in the future are better sampled at 1.5-to-1 or 2-to-1.

For very small images [less than 3" (7.6cm)], I suggest scanning at a 2-to-1 ratio. The halftone looks better, the size of the file isn't significantly bigger and you can enlarge and/or crop the image a bit if you decide to later.

Optimal spi settings at 1.5 sampling ratio

SPI	HALFTONE SCREEN FREQUENCY				
	65	85	100	133	150
75	77%	59%	50%	38%	33%
90	92%	71%	60%	45%	40%
100	103%	78%	67%	50%	44%
120	123%	94%	80%	60%	53%
150	154%	118%	100%	75%	67%
180	185%	141%	120%	90%	80%
200	205%	157%	133%	100%	89%
210	215%	165%	140%	105%	93%
240	246%	188%	160%	120%	107%
270	277%	212%	180%	135%	120%
300	308%	235%	200%	150%	133%
360	369%	282%	240%	180%	160%
400	410%	314%	267%	201%	178%
480	492%	376%	320%	241%	213%
600	615%	471%	400%	301%	267%
800	821%	627%	533%	401%	356%
1,200	1,231%	941%	800%	602%	533%

Optimal spi settings at 2.0 sampling ratio

	HALFTONE SCREEN FREQUENCY				
SPI	65	85	100	133	150
75	58%	44%	38%	28%	25%
90	69%	53%	45%	34%	30%
100	77%	59%	50%	38%	33%
120	92%	71%	60%	45%	40%
150	115%	88%	75%	56%	50%
180	138%	106%	90%	68%	60%
200	154%	118%	100%	75%	67%
210	162%	124%	105%	79%	70%
240	185%	141%	120%	90%	80%
270	208%	159%	135%	102%	90%
300	231%	176%	150%	113%	100%
360	277%	212%	180%	135%	120%
400	308%	235%	200%	150%	133%
480	369%	282%	240%	180%	160%
600	462%	353%	300%	226%	200%
800	615%	471%	400%	301%	267%
1,200	923%	706%	600%	451%	400%

Scanning Formula

Here's a formula that can help you calculate the appropriate number of samples per inch (spi) when scanning:

Halftone Screen (lpi) x Sampling Rate (spi) = Output Resolution (ppi)

Magnification/100 x Output Resolution (ppi) = Target Scanning Resolution (spi)

Here's how it works if you want to scan an image at a sample rate of 1.5 and output it to a 150-line screen for final reproduction at 80 percent of its original size: Output resolution is 150 x 1.5 = 225 ppi. Since the reduction is 80 percent, the target scanning resolution is 80/100 x 225 = 180 spi.

I created the tables on this and the previous two pages with a spreadsheet program using the formula above for each cell. You may be able to create other application-specific tables for your own use or even program a hand calculator to do the same.

Note: An important downside to 2-to-1 scanning is that film output takes longer, and in many cases you are charged extra for the RIP time. That 1.5-to-1 ratio looks better all the time, doesn't it? On the upside, you can change your mind and enlarge the picture much more if you have 2-to-1 sampling. As I said, for important images 2-to-1 is a good bet.

Scan Calculator

The scan calculator shown below can be used by visiting our web site at http://www.hsdesign.com/scancalc.

SCAN CALCULATOR

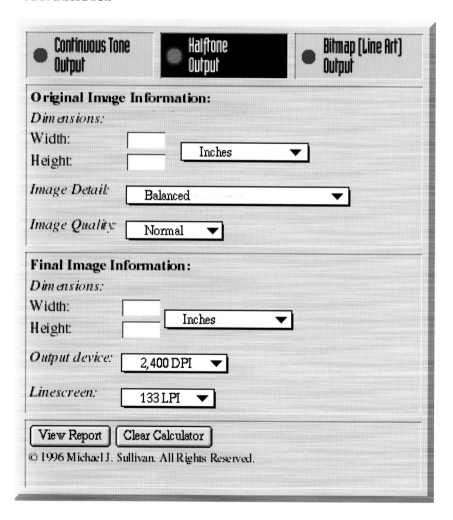

Legal and Ethical Issues

Who Owns This Image?

Scanning an image that somebody else has created is, by legal definition, reproducing an image—an act that requires the granting of reproduction rights by the image's owner. Once the image is scanned, digitally altering it is creating, by legal definition, a derivative work. Creating a derivative work requires permission from the owner of the original who then grants adaptation rights.

A host of issues surrounds which images can and cannot legally be used for scanning purposes. Understanding these issues can prevent you from being sued. The legal areas that may cumulatively or separately affect your right to scan a given image are:

- Copyright
- Moral rights
- Trademark
- Trade secret

Copyright

The most widely used, and misunderstood, law regarding the use of images is the copyright. Under current U.S. law, an image doesn't have to have a copyright notice (the © symbol) to be protected by copyright.

The idea of a copyright is to give an artist exclusive rights to profit from a work that he or she created for a set period of time. After the term has expired, the copyrighted work automatically falls into the public domain. Thus, the public has a right to use a work once the original artist has been given fair chance to make money from it.

Images created prior to 1978 become public domain twenty-eight years after their creation, unless their copyrights have been renewed, which entitles them to an additional forty-seven years of protection. Images created on or after January 1, 1978, are covered under copyright protection until seventy-five years after their creation. Unpublished works are protected for fifty years after a copyright holder's death.

Using an image, including scanning it, without a license from the copyright owner is an infringement of the copyright. Infringers may be sued by the copyright owner or heirs for damages, legal fees and more.

What's Copyright Free?

- Clip Art Images—You can scan any clip art images that are clearly marked as "copyright free" images.
- Old Images—Basically anything seventy-five years old or more (i.e., 28 + 47) is safe to scan, although other protection may apply. Images twenty-eight years old or older may also be useable, but you should first determine if a copyright extension was applied for before you scan such an image.
- Public Domain—Any image that has been deliberately given to the public is OK to use. The problem is determining which images qualify. Note that most NASA images are available to the public, with proper credit, since your tax dollars paid for them. But the problem is that if you scan a NASA image from a magazine or book you may be violating that publisher's copyright since they may have enhanced the original image in ways that you are unaware of.

Moral Rights

A new twist to the copyright law is the passage of the Visual Artists Rights Act of 1990. In effect, this law gives an artist the right to claim authorship of a work, the right to prevent associating an artist's name with a work that artist didn't create and the right to prevent any intentional distortion or modification of a work. Using such protection, artists may prevent you from changing, in any way, a scan of their work, even if that work is in the public domain. Thus, if you photograph an artist's painting, scan it and modify it in an image manipulation program, then you may be violating the artist's moral rights. Again, if it isn't yours, get permission first.

Trademarks

You should also be aware of another legal protection device—the trademark. Corporate logos are usually protected under trademark law and shouldn't be scanned or used without permission. Watch out for familiar graphics or characters—Snoopy, Dilbert, Mickey Mouse and Opus are all trademarked, and using their images, even innocently, can be hazardous to your pocketbook. Some trademark holders are particularly litigious.

Trade Secrets

Trade secrets protection offers perpetual protection as long as the information being copied remains a secret. Copying plans, drawings, diagrams, lists, documents and even certain photographs that belong to a corporation may expose you to a lawsuit—especially if you move to another corporation and take those copies with you. Your former employer can enjoin you from going to work for a competitor, especially if you signed a nondisclosure agreement.

Ethics

To be fair, you should always attempt to get permission to use someone else's image. You might be surprised—you may get to use it for free if your cause is good and the originator feels sympathetic. On the other hand, if you are making beaucoup bucks on a project, then it is reasonable to expect to share some of the proceeds with others.

For many people, taking pictures, producing art and creating illustrations is their only means of earning a living. Additionally, an entire industry of support people—from photo labs to artists' reps to publishers—depends on the work that photographers, artists and illustrators create. This community is damaged each time someone makes a copy of something that belongs to someone else. It is up to you to respect the work of others when scanning, as much as you expect others to respect your own.

How to Protect Your Own Images From Plagiarism

Your work is your copyrighted material and it doesn't necessarily have to be registered with the U.S. Copyright Office to be protected under copyright laws. Significantly altering or modifying a scanned public domain image qualifies as a new, derivative work and is automatically protected. All pictorial, graphic and three-dimensional artwork can be copyrighted. You can discourage others from plagiarizing your work by including a copyright on your original.

To register your work, contact the U.S. Copyright Office, Library of Congress, LM 455, Washington, DC 20559, (202) 707-3000. You can also request a number of publications prepared by the copyright office. Circular 1 is Copyright Basics, Circular 2 lists all other publications. Circulars 22 and 23 cover searching copyright office records to determine the copyright status and/or ownership of a work. You can also visit the U.S. Copyright Office on the Web at http://lcweb.loc.gov/copyright/.

For More Information

AMERICAN SOCIETY OF MEDIA PHOTOGRAPHERS, 14 Washington Rd., Suite 502, Princeton Junction, NJ 08550, (609) 799-8330, http://www2.asmp.org

The society offers several pertinent publications: *Membership Directory* ($18.00), *Copyright Guide for Photographers* ($5.00) and *Stock Photography Handbook (*$29.95), which includes a list of stock picture agencies.

THE ART LAW PRIMER: A MANUAL FOR VISUAL ARTISTS ($9.95) by Linda F. Pinkerton and John T. Guardalabene, published by Lyons & Burford, 31 W. Twenty-first St., New York, NY 10010, (212) 620-9580

An introduction to all sorts of legal areas that photographers and other visual artists are likely to encounter, including an excellent chapter on copyright.

GRAPHIC ARTISTS GUILD, 90 John St., Suite 403, New York, NY 10038-3202, (212) 791-3400, http://www.gag.org

The Graphic Artists Guild offers a number of publications, including *Ethical Guide to Graphic Design and Illustration Services* ($29.95). The Guild is a strong advocate for the rights of visual artists.

LEGAL GUIDE FOR THE VISUAL ARTIST ($19.95) by Tad Crawford, published by Allworth Press, distributed by F&W Publications, Inc., 1507 Dana Ave., Cincinnati, OH 45207, (513) 531-2690

This is an introduction to all sorts of legal areas that photographers, illustrators and other visual artists are likely to encounter. Includes examples of legal contracts and provides an excellent overview on copyright.

MULTIMEDIA: LAW & PRACTICE ($125.80) by Michael D. Scott, published by Prentice Hall Law & Business, 270 Sylvan Ave., Englewood Cliffs, NJ 07632, (800) 223-0231 (1993)

An excellent, easy-to-read survey of the legal issues involved in using material for multimedia in regard to copyrights, moral rights, trademarks and patent law.

PICTURE RESEARCH: A PRACTICAL GUIDE ($37.95) by John Schultz and Barbara Schultz, published by Van Nostrand Reinhold, 7625 Empire Dr., Florence, KY 41042, (800) 842-3636

Covering the background and techniques of acquiring reproduction rights and researching ownership for photographs and other pictures, this highly recommended book includes chapters on copyright law as well as electronic publishing.

Glossary

A/D CONVERTER—Analog-to-digital converter. An electronic device that converts an analog signal, such as that generated by a CCD, into digital information.

ADDITIVE PRIMARIES—Another name for red, green and blue. Called additive because when all three are combined they create pure white.

ALIASING—*See* **JAGGIES**.

ANALOG—Continuously variable signals or data, as opposed to digital.

BIT—Binary digit. The basic unit of information that all computers use to manipulate data. The value of a bit (0 or 1) represents a two-way choice, such as yes/no, on/off or black/white.

BIT DEPTH—The amount of tone data per sample expressed in number of bits. Typical bit depths are 1 (for line art), 8 (for grayscale) and 24 (for color images).

BITMAP—Originally a term used to describe a memory model where each bit in screen memory was "mapped" to a corresponding screen pixel, hence the term *bitmapped*. Today it is used universally to describe all manner of pixel-oriented displays, from 1 bit (true bitmapped) to grayscale (8 bits per pixel) to full color (16 or 24 bits per pixel).

BLACK POINT—*See* **SHADOW POINT**.

BRIGHTNESS—The intensity of light reflected from a print, transmitted by a transparency or emitted by a pixel.

BYTE—A computer term equal to 256 levels of information (2^8). Also, the number of bits used to represent a character. 1 byte equals 8 bits. A standard unit of measure for file size. *See also* **GIGABYTE**, **KILOBYTE**, **MEGABYTE** and **TERABYTE**.

CCD—Charge-coupled device. A light-sensitive electronic device that emits an electrical signal proportional to the amount of light striking it. Used in scanners and video cameras.

CD-ROM—Compact disc read-only memory. A CD-ROM drive uses the CD (compact disc) format as a computer storage medium. One CD can store approximately 640 megabytes of data and other mixed media.

CHANNEL—Analogous to a plate in the printing process, a channel is the foundation of a computer image. Some image types have only one channel, while others have several, with up to sixteen channels.

CIE—Commission Internationale de l'Eclairage. An international standards committee that defined the de facto standard color model used in all color management systems.

CMS—Color management system. A comprehensive hardware/software solution for maintaining color fidelity of an image from scanner to monitor to printer.

CMYK—Cyan, magenta, yellow, black. The subtractive primary colors plus black, also known as process colors, used in color printing. *See also* **SUBTRACTIVE PRIMARIES**.

COLOR CAST—The effect of one color dominating the overall look of an image. Often caused by improper exposure, wrong film type or unusual lighting conditions when shooting the original image. In scanning, also caused by the sometimes unpredictable interaction between an image and a scanner.

COLOR SEPARATION—An image that has been converted or "separated" from RGB into the four process colors. *See also* **CMYK**.

COMPRESSION—Algorithms used to create smaller file sizes of stored images. There are two kinds of compression: **LOSSLESS** and **LOSSY**.

CONTRAST—The difference in brightness between the lightest and darkest tones in an image. Also, a steep region in a tone curve.

CROP—To permanently discard unwanted information in the perimeter area of an image.

DCS—Desktop color separation. A five-file EPS file format consisting of four high-resolution color separations and a fifth position-only file for placement within documents.

DECOMPRESSION—The opposite of compression. Decompressed images are as big as and have the same resolution as the original image before compression.

DEFAULT—A setting in a computer program that takes

effect if no changes are made.

DENSITY—The measure of light blocking (in the case of transparencies) or absorption (in the case of prints), expressed logarithmically. Typical slides have a density of 3.0 while typical prints have a density of 2.0.

DESCREENING—The technique of eliminating moiré patterns when scanning.

DIGITAL—Discrete data made up of steps or levels, as opposed to analog.

DITHERING—A technique of using patterns of dots or pixels to create the effect of an intermediate tonal value.

DMAX—The maximum density in an image. *See also* **SHADOW POINT.**

DMIN—The minimum density in an image. *See also* **WHITE POINT.**

DOT GAIN—The effect of ink spread and absorption into paper during printing resulting in darker tones, especially midtones.

DPI—Dots per inch. A measure of the output resolution produced by laser printers or imagesetters. *See also* **LPI.**

DRIVER—A small software module that contains specific information needed by an application to control or "drive" a peripheral such as a monitor, scanner or printer.

DRUM SCANNER—A high-end scanning device, utilizing PMT technology, used to digitize prints, transparencies and artwork.

EPS—Encapsulated PostScript. A subset of the PostScript page description language that allows any single-page artwork, be it line art or image data, to be saved and placed into any other EPS-compatible document. *See also* **DCS** and **POSTSCRIPT.**

EPS 5—Another term for DCS.

EXPOSURE—Defines the overall brightness of an image resulting from a combination of time and intensity of light allowed to the film.

FILE—A named collection of binary information stored as an apparent unit on a secondary storage medium such as a computer disk drive.

FILM RECORDER—A device that renders digital data onto analog film. Typical film sizes are 35mm and 4" x 5".

FLATBED SCANNER—A popular type of desktop scanner so

called because of its glass platen, or "bed," upon which originals are placed to be scanned.

FPO—For position only. Typically a low-resolution image positioned in a document only to be replaced later with a higher resolution version of the same image.

FRAME GRABBER—A device that captures and digitizes a single frame of a video sequence. Typical resolution is 640 x 480 samples.

GAMMA CORRECTION—The measure of contrast that results in lightening or darkening the midtone regions of an image. Also, the amount by which midtones need to be adjusted on a monitor.

GIF—Pronounced "jif," GIF is the de facto standard image format for online uses, especially the World Wide Web.

GIGABYTE—Equivalent to exactly 1,073,741,824 bytes of information (2^{30}).

GRAYSCALE—A continuous tone image made up of a number of shades of gray. *See also* **MONOCHROME.**

HALFTONE—A technique of converting a continuous-tone (grayscale) image into variable-sized spots representing the individual tones of the image.

HALO—A consequence of using too high a setting of radius in unsharp masking. The effect is one of a light region surrounding the perimeter of a darker region.

HARD DISK—A secondary storage medium for computer files. A place to store scanned images.

HIGH KEY—An image that is primarily composed of light tones.

HIGHLIGHT—The lightest desirable tone in an image. The tonal value in an image above which all tones are rendered pure white. *See also* **DMIN** and **WHITE POINT.**

HISTOGRAM—A graphic representation of the number of samples corresponding to each tone in an image. *See also* **TONE CURVES.**

HUE—The main differentiating attribute of a color. The wavelength of light that represents a color.

ICON—In a graphical user interface, an on-screen symbol that represents a program file or computer function.

IMAGESETTER—A high-end device for taking rasterized data (*see* **RIP**) and exposing film used for printing processes.

INTERPOLATION—The technique of estimating the tonal value that lies between two known tone samples. Used for enlarging an existing image. Also used when capturing an image during the scanning process to achieve higher than optical resolution.

INVERTING—Creating a negative of an image.

IT8—An industry standard color reference target used to calibrate scanners and printers. Many color management systems use IT8 targets.

JAGGIES—The pixelated or stair-step appearance of low-resolution computer-generated images.

JPEG—Joint Photographic Experts Group. An industry standard lossy form of compression for image data. JPEG offers one of the best compression schemes available.

KILOBYTE—Equivalent to exactly 1,024 bytes of information (2^{10}).

LASER PRINTER—A printing device using electrostatic toner to create an image derived from page description information.

LINE ART—Images made up of only pure black-and-white data. Also a mode of capturing such images.

LOSSY—A technique of compressing an image by eliminating redundant or unnecessary information.

LOW KEY—An image that is primarily composed of dark tones.

LPI—Lines per inch. A measure of the frequency of a half-tone screen used in printing. The archaic, and now misleading, term *line* harkens back to the diffraction line etchings used to create analog halftones.

LZW—Lempel-Ziv-Welch. A popular lossless image compression algorithm.

MATRIX—A grid of horizontal and vertical cells. For example, video cameras use a matrix of CCDs.

MEGABYTE—Equivalent to exactly 1,048,576 bytes of information (2^{20}).

MIDTONE—The range of tones in an image located approximately halfway between highlights and shadows.

MODEM—MOdulator/DEModulator. An electronic device used to convert a computer's digital signal to an analog one and vice versa. The result is a signal that can be transmitted over telephone lines.

MOIRÉ—An undesirable interference pattern in color printing often resulting from misaligned or improper screen angles. Also created when previously halftoned images are scanned.

MONITOR—The device that produces an on-screen display. Synonymous with video display unit. There are three types of monitors: black and white, grayscale and color.

MONOCHROME—An image made up of various shades of one hue. *See also* **GRAYSCALE**.

NEWTON RINGS—A pattern of concentric, multicolored rings occasionally introduced in a scanned image by contact of transparency film with the glass platen in a scanner.

NOISE—Extraneous or random samples introduced into a scanned image via the electronic components of a scanner.

OCR—Optical character recognition. Software that uses pattern recognition to distinguish character shapes in a bitmapped image. Typically used with scanners.

OFFSET LITHOGRAPHY—A commonly used printing process utilizing an intermediate blanket cylinder to transfer or "offset" an image from the plate to the paper.

OPTICAL RESOLUTION—The true number of discrete samples per inch that a scanner can distinguish in an image.

OVERSAMPLING—Scanning an image at higher than 8 bits per channel. Used for high-end image manipulation—greater bit depths allow for greater image fidelity. Available from mid- to high-level scanning equipment.

OVERSCANNING—Scanning an image at a higher resolution than is necessary. Used for archiving images for later use.

PICT—A Macintosh-based format for storage and exchange of graphic documents, containing bitmapped and/or object-based images.

PIXEL—Picture element. One of the individual elements that make up a video monitor's image area. Typical monitor pixel resolutions are 640 x 480, 800 x 600, 1,024 x 768.

PLATEN—The glass scanning region on a flatbed scanner.

PMT—Photo multiplier tube. The kind of technology used in drum scanners.

PNG—Portable Network Graphics. Pronounced "ping." A new graphic file format, especially suited for the World Wide Web, destined to take the place of GIF.

POSTSCRIPT—A robust, general-purpose page description

language that has become the de facto standard in the prepress industry. Used in most all imagesetters and many laser printers.

PPI—Pixels per inch. The frequency of the number of samples used to display an image on a computer monitor.

PRESCAN—A quick, low-resolution preview scan of an image to be scanned.

PRIMARY COLOR—A base color used to create other colors. Examples are red, magenta, green, yellow, blue and cyan.

PROCESS COLOR—The CMY primary colors (plus black) used in printing to produce the widest spectrum of printable colors. *See also* **COLOR SEPARATION.**

PROFILE—The compiled color characteristics of a known device, such as a monitor or scanner, as used with a color management system.

QUARTER TONES—Tones in an image that lie between midtones and highlights. Three-quarter tones are tones between midtones and shadows.

RAM—Random-access memory. The memory a computer needs to store the information it is processing at any given moment. The larger the amount of RAM, the larger the file size and the greater the speed with which they can be processed.

RASTER—A bitmapped representation of data. *See also* **RIP.**

RESAMPLE—To change the resolution (and the resulting file size) of an image. Resampling to a higher resolution introduces more data through interpolation.

RESOLUTION—The output measurement of an image, expressed in dots per inch (dpi), pixels per inch (ppi) or lines per inch (lpi).

RGB—Red, green, blue. The additive primary colors used in computer monitors and image recorders.

RIP—Raster image processor. The software/hardware device that interprets output data (such as page description information) to create a bitmapped image made up of output dots and deliver that image to a print engine.

SAMPLE—The smallest, discrete amount of data captured by a scanner. Expressed in bit depths of 1, 8 or 24 bits.

SATURATION—The amount of gray in a color. Less gray results in more saturation.

SCREEN FREQUENCY—*See* **HALFTONE, LPI.**

SCSI—Small computer system interface. A standard that allows communication between computers and peripheral devices.

SEPARATIONS—*See* **COLOR SEPARATION.**

SHADOW POINT—The samples in an image that will print the darkest tone possible on the intended output device. Tonal values below this will print pure black. *See also* **DMAX.**

SHARPENING—A technique of accentuating the contrast between all areas of tonal difference within an image.

SPECTRAL HIGHLIGHT—Pure white with no tone. Spectral highlights within an image should not be used for Set White Point.

SPI—Samples per inch. The measurement used throughout this book that refers to the number of image data samples captured per inch, as opposed to the terms *dpi* and *ppi* (often used incorrectly), which are measurements of output.

SUBTRACTIVE PRIMARIES—Another term for cyan, magenta and yellow. Called subtractive because when all three are combined they absorb all light (theoretically) and create black. *See also* **CMYK.**

TERABYTE—Equivalent to exactly 1,099,511,627,776 bytes of information (2^{40}).

THRESHOLD—The tonal value, used when scanning line art or converting grayscale images to bitmapped, above which is rendered white and below which is rendered black. Typically expressed in percentage of gray.

TIFF—Tag image file format. A popular file format used for storing images. TIFF formats support a wide range of color models and bit depths.

TONE CURVES—A linear graphic representation of the mapping of input tones to output tones. *See also* **HISTOGRAM.**

UNSHARP MASKING—Also known as USM. A technique of accentuating the contrast at border areas of significant tonal difference within an image. With proper controls, USM will only sharpen areas of important detail. *See also* **SHARPENING.**

WHITE POINT—The samples in an image that will print the lightest tone possible of the intended output device. Tonal values above this will print pure white. Not to be confused with spectral highlight. *See also* **DMIN.**

Permissions

Page 8, Diagram courtesy of Agfa Divisions, Miles Inc. Used by permission.

Page 47, Digital camera courtesy of Apple Computer, Inc. Photographer: John Greenleigh. Used by permission.

Page 121, Copyright © ArtScans. Photographer: Graham Nash. Used by permission.

Page 123, Copyright © Darryl Curran. Used by permission.

Page 125, Copyright © Katrin Eismann. Used by permission.

Page 127, Copyright © Eric Dinyer. Used by permission.

Page 129, Copyright © NancyScans, Inc. Used by permission.

Page 131, Copyright © Bob and Lois Schlowsky. Used by permission.

Page 134, Photo courtesy of Binuscan, Inc.; photo courtesy of Jetsoft Development Company; photo courtesy of Monaco Systems, Inc.

Page 135, Photo courtesy of Stalker Software.

Page 136, Photo courtesy of Xerox Corporation.

Page 137, Photo courtesy of Apple Computer, Inc. Photographer: John Greenleigh; photo courtesy of Eastman Kodak Company; photo courtesy of Agfa Division Bayer Corporation.

Page 138, Photo courtesy of Agfa Division Bayer Corporation; photo courtesy of Apple Computer, Inc.; photo courtesy of Epson America, Inc.; photo courtesy of Hewlett-Packard Company.

Page 139, Photo courtesy of Microtek Lab, Inc.

Page 140, Photo courtesy of UMAX Technologies, Inc.; photo courtesy of Agfa Division Bayer Corporation; photo courtesy of Ana Tech/Intergraph; photo courtesy of Howtek, Inc.

Page 141, Photo courtesy of ICG North America; photo courtesy of Imapro Corporation; photo courtesy of Optronics International; photo courtesy of Scanview, Inc.; photo courtesy of Scitex; photo courtesy of Screen USA; photo courtesy of Umax Technologies.

Page 142, Photo courtesy of Vision Shape; photo courtesy of Eastman Kodak Company; photo courtesy of Nikon Electronic Imaging.

143, Photo courtesy of Calcomp; photo courtesy of Hewlett-Packard Company.

Index

More Great Books for Knock-Out Graphic Design!

1998 Artist's & Graphic Designer's Market—This marketing tool for fine artists and graphic designers includes listings of 2,500 buyers across the country and helpful advice on selling and showing your work from top art and design professionals. #10514/$24.99/786 pages

WWW Design: Web Pages from Around the World—Use the most innovative designs and graphics on the Web today to inspire your own Website design. Includes interactive CD-ROM (Mac/PC). #30960/$49.99/160 pages/300 color images

Graphic Design America—Peek into the portfolios of 38 of the best up-and-coming U.S. designers and design firms. Discover what's new and innovative and how your work can rise above the rest. #30962/$49.99/256 pages/400 color illus.

Graphic Design: New York 2—Take a look at 38 stand-out portfolios from the city that put graphic design on the map. Studios like Louise Fili, Desgrippes Gobe and Carin Goldberg are represented. #30948/$49.99/256 pages/400 color illus.

The Complete Guide to Eco-Friendly Design—59 real-world case studies reveal both the technical information AND the creative inspiration you'll need to produce earth-friendly printed pieces. #30847/$29.99/144 pages/118 color illus.

Digital Type—Type becomes essential design elements in more than 100 examples of cutting-edge type from leading design firms. Use for magazines, brochures, ads, posters, many others. #30956/$34.99/144 pages/200 color images

Great T-shirt Graphics 3—Showcases the latest trends in more than 350 silk-screened, airbrushed, and printed T-shirts from top international designers. Includes interactive CD-ROM (Mac/PC) with 500 designs from vols. 1-3. #30958/$44.99/160 pages/350 color images

Package & Label Design—More than 300 of the best new, innovative packaging and label designs from top international designers. Includes interactive CD-ROM (Mac/PC) with 700 archive images. #30989/$44.99/160 pages/300 color images

Using Design Basics to Get Creative Results—60 real-world, full-color projects show you how to create powerful designs built on foundations of basic principles. Each section ends with helpful exercises and self-test questions. #30828/$29.99/144 pages/125 illus.

Getting Started in Multimedia Design—Here's creative advice, business tips and other secrets to success from accomplished media designer Gary Olsen. #30886/$29.99/144 pages/176 color illus./paperback

Clip Art Smart: How to Choose and Use Digital Clip Art—Shows you how to effectively use clip art to improve design and save time and money. Includes interactive CD-ROM (Mac/PC) with 500 copyright-free images. #30994/$39.99/144 pages/200 color images

Graphic Design: Inspiration and Innovations 2—When circumstances conspire against you, get inspired by these case studies of the best of design done under the worst of circumstances.

Helps you see how creative thinking can turn near-disaster into triumph. #30930/$29.99/144 pages/177 color illus.

Even More Great Design Using 1, 2 & 3 Colors—When budgets are tight, reach for this book. 170 innovative designs using limited colors on posters, stationery, packaging, annual reports, and more. #30955/$39.95/192 pages/300 color illus.

Graphic Design Basics: Pricing, Estimating & Budgeting—Make money with confidence using simple steps to boost the profitability of your design company and make things run a lot smoother. You'll learn money-managing essentials that every self-employed designer needs to succeed—from writing estimates to sticking to budgets. #30744/$27.99/128 pages/ 47 color, 49 b&w illus.

The Graphic Designer's Sourcebook—Find everything you need to run your business and to pull off your most innovative concepts. With names and phone numbers for more than 1,000 suppliers of unusual and everyday services and materials, this reference will save you hours of rooting for information. Listings include type, packaging, studio equipment, illustration, photography and much more! #30760/$24.99/160 pages/18 b&w illus./paperback

Fresh Ideas in Brochure Design—Make your design memorable with inspiration from this collection of cutting-edge sampling of today's best brochure design from 69 top studios around the country. #30929/$31.99/160 pages/298 color illus.

Graphic Design Basics: Creating Logos & Letterheads—Using 14 creativity-sparking, step-by-step demonstrations, Jennifer Place shows you how to make logos, letterheads and business cards that speak out about a client and pack a visual punch. #30616/$27.99/128 pages/ 110 color, 125 b&w illus.

Best Small Budget Self-Promotions—Get an inside look at the best of low-budget promotion with this showcase of more than 150 pieces that make clients stop and take notice. Included are examples of distinctive identity systems, unconventional self-promotions, pro bono work and more! Plus, you'll find costs and quantities, cost-cutting tricks and the story behind the designs. #30747/$28.99/136 pages/195 illus.

Creativity for Graphic Designers—If you're burned-out or just plain stuck for ideas, this book will help you spark your creativity and find the best idea for any project. #30659/$29.99/144 pages/169 color illus.

Designer's Guide to Marketing—Good design by itself isn't enough! Discover the key steps you must make to achieve the success your work deserves. Easy-to-understand marketing know-how to help you win clients and keep them. #30932/$29.99/144 pages/112 color illus.

Graphic Design Tricks & Techniques—Your quick reference to over 300 expert time- and cost-saving ideas from top studios. Get fantastic results in design, production, printing and more. #30919/$27.99/144 pages/19 b&w, 99 color illus.

The Best Seasonal Promotions—Get inspired with this exceptional collection of more than 150 fully illustrated promotions for every holiday and season of the year. Includes info on concept, cost, print run and production specs. #30931/$29.99/144 pages/196 color illus.

Graphic Artists Guild Handbook of Pricing & Ethical Guidelines, 9th Edition—You'll get practical advice on how to negotiate fees, the ins and outs of trade practices, the latest tax advice and more. #30896/$29.95/328 pages/paperback

Graphic Design Basics: Creating Brochures and Booklets—Detailed demonstrations show you precisely how to plan, design and produce everything from a church bulletin to a four-color brochure. Plus, a full-color gallery of 20 well-designed brochures and booklets will give you loads of inspiration. #30568/$26.99/128 pages/ 60 color, 145 b&w illus.

Fresh Ideas in Letterhead & Business Card Design 3—A great idea-sparker for your letterhead, envelope and business card designs. 120 sets shown large, in color, and with notes on concepts, production and costs. #30885/$29.99/144 pages/325 color illus.

Fresh Ideas in Promotion 2—Volume 2 in this inspiring series of the best new work in promotion. Includes captions with concept, cost, print run and production specs. #30829/$29.99/144 pages/160 color illus.

Other fine North Light Books are available from your local bookstore, art supply store, or direct from the publisher. Write to the address below for a FREE catalog of all North Light Books. To order books directly from the publisher, include $3.50 postage and handling for one book, $1.50 for each additional book. Ohio residents add 6% sales tax. Allow 30 days for delivery.

North Light Books
1507 Dana Avenue
Cincinnati, Ohio 45207

VISA/MasterCard orders call TOLL-FREE
1-800-289-0963

Prices subject to change without notice.   Stock may be limited on some books.

Write to this address for information on *The Artist's Magazine*, *HOW* magazine, North Light Books, Graphic Design Book Club, North Light Art School, and Betterway Books. To receive information on art or design competitions, send a SASE to Dept. BOI, Attn: Competition Coordinator, at the above address.   8548